LIVING BEAUTIFULLY
WITH UNCERTAINTY AND CHANGE

Books by Pema Chödrön

Always Maintain a Joyful Mind: *And Other Lojong Teachings on Awakening Compassion and Fearlessness*

Awakening Loving-Kindness

Comfortable with Uncertainty: *108 Teachings on Cultivating Fearlessness and Compassion*

No Time to Lose: *A Timely Guide to the Way of the Bodhisattva*

The Places That Scare You: *A Guide to Fearlessness in Difficult Times*

The Pocket Pema Chödrön

Practicing Peace in Times of War

Start Where You Are: *A Guide to Compassionate Living*

Taking the Leap: *Freeing Ourselves from Old Habits and Fears*

When Things Fall Apart: *Heart Advice for Difficult Times*

The Wisdom of No Escape: *And the Path of Loving-Kindness*

LIVING
BEAUTIFULLY
WITH UNCERTAINTY
AND CHANGE

Pema Chödrön

Edited by Joan Duncan Oliver

SHAMBHALA
Boston & London 2012

SHAMBHALA PUBLICATIONS, INC.
Horticultural Hall
300 Massachusetts Avenue
Boston, Massachusetts 02115
www.shambhala.com

9 8 7 6 5 4 3 2 1

First Edition
Printed in the United States of America

♾ This edition is printed on acid-free paper that meets the American National Standards Institute Z39.48 Standard.
♻ This book is printed on 30% postconsumer recycled paper. For more information please visit www.shambhala.com.

Distributed in the United States by Random House, Inc.,
and in Canada by Random House of Canada Ltd

Designed by Daniel Urban-Brown

Library of Congress Cataloging-in-Publication Data
Chödrön, Pema.
Living beautifully with uncertainty and change / Pema Chödrön;
edited by Joan Duncan Oliver.—First Edition.
pages cm
ISBN 978-1-59030-963-6 (hardback)
1. Religious life—Buddhism. 2. Uncertainty—Religious aspects—Buddhism. 3. Buddhism—Doctrines. I. Oliver, Joan Duncan, editor. II. Title.
BQ5405.C45 2012
294.3'444—dc23
2012005546

May the aspirations of
Chögyam Trungpa Rinpoche
The Druk Sakyong
The Dorje Dradül of Mukpo
be rapidly fulfilled

Contents

The Third Commitment: Committing to Embrace the World Just as It Is

Concluding Words

Preface

THE TEACHINGS IN THIS BOOK were given at Gampo Abbey, a Tibetan Buddhist monastery in Cape Breton, Nova Scotia, in 2009, during the six-week winter retreat known as Yarne. They are loosely based on traditional Buddhist material pertaining to what are called the Three Vows: the Pratimoksha Vow, the Bodhisattva Vow, and the Samaya Vow.

Generally when this material is presented, it is with the understanding that these vows would be taken formally with a teacher. The Pratimoksha Vow would come first, followed later by the Bodhisattva Vow. And finally, if the student decided to work closely with a Vajrayana master, he or she would take the Samaya Vow.

Here, I have chosen to teach these vows in a more general way, presenting them as three commitments that anyone of any religion—or no religion—can make as a way of relating to the impermanent, ever-shifting nature of our life experience, as a way of using our everyday experience to wake up, perk up, lighten up, and be more loving and conscious of other beings.

May this admittedly unconventional approach to a traditional subject be helpful and encouraging to all who read this book. And may some readers even become curious about the traditional way of taking these vows as part of the Buddhist journey to enlightenment.

—Pema Chödrön

The Overview

Living is a form of not being sure, not knowing what next
or how. The moment you know how, you begin to die a
little. The artist never entirely knows. We guess. We may
be wrong, but we take leap after leap in the dark.

—AGNES DE MILLE

1

The Fundamental Ambiguity
of Being Human

Life is like stepping into a boat that is about to sail out to
sea and sink.

— SHUNRYU SUZUKI ROSHI

As HUMAN BEINGS we share a tendency to scramble for
certainty whenever we realize that everything around us is
in flux. In difficult times the stress of trying to find solid
ground—something predictable and safe to stand on—
seems to intensify. But in truth, the very nature of our existence is forever in flux. Everything keeps changing, whether
we're aware of it or not.

What a predicament! We seem doomed to suffer simply
because we have a deep-seated fear of how things really are.
Our attempts to find lasting pleasure, lasting security, are
at odds with the fact that we're part of a dynamic system in
which everything and everyone is in process.

So this is where we find ourselves: right in the middle
of a dilemma. And it leaves us with some provocative
questions: How can we live wholeheartedly in the face of
impermanence, knowing that one day we're going to die?
What is it like to realize we can never completely and finally get it all together? Is it possible to increase our tolerance for instability and change? How can we make friends

with unpredictability and uncertainty—and embrace them as vehicles to transform our lives?

The Buddha called impermanence one of the three distinguishing marks of our existence, an incontrovertible fact of life. But it's something we seem to resist pretty strongly. We think that if only we did this or didn't do that, somehow we could achieve a secure, dependable, controllable life. How disappointed we are when things don't work out quite the way we planned.

Not long ago, I read an interview with the war correspondent Chris Hedges in which he used a phrase that seemed like a perfect description of our situation: "the moral ambiguity of human existence." This refers, I think, to an essential choice that confronts us all: whether to cling to the false security of our fixed ideas and tribal views, even though they bring us only momentary satisfaction, or to overcome our fear and make the leap to living an authentic life. That phrase, "the moral ambiguity of human existence," resonated strongly with me because it's what I've been exploring for years: How can we relax and have a genuine, passionate relationship with the fundamental uncertainty, the groundlessness of being human?

My first teacher, Chögyam Trungpa, used to talk about the fundamental anxiety of being human. This anxiety or queasiness in the face of impermanence isn't something that afflicts just a few of us; it's an all-pervasive state that human beings share. But rather than being disheartened by the ambiguity, the uncertainty of life, what if we accepted it and relaxed into it? What if we said, "Yes, this is the way it is; this is what it means to be human," and decided to sit down and enjoy the ride?

Happily, the Buddha gave many instructions on how to do

just this. Among these instructions are what are known in the Tibetan Buddhist tradition as the Three Vows, or Three Commitments. These are three methods for embracing the chaotic, unstable, dynamic, challenging nature of our situation as a path to awakening. The first of the commitments, traditionally called the Pratimoksha Vow, is the foundation for personal liberation. This is a commitment to doing our best to not cause harm with our actions or words or thoughts, a commitment to being good to each other. It provides a structure within which we learn to work with our thoughts and emotions and to refrain from speaking or acting out of confusion. The next step toward being comfortable with groundlessness is a commitment to helping others. Traditionally called the Bodhisattva Vow, it is a commitment to dedicate our lives to keeping our hearts and minds open and to nurturing our compassion with the longing to ease the suffering of the world. The last of the Three Commitments, traditionally known as the Samaya Vow, is a resolve to embrace the world just as it is, without bias. It is a commitment to see everything we encounter, good and bad, pleasant and painful, as a manifestation of awakened energy. It is a commitment to see anything and everything as a means by which we can awaken further.

But what does the fundamental ambiguity of being human mean in terms of day-to-day life? Above all, it means understanding that everything changes. As Shantideva, an eighth-century Buddhist master, wrote in *The Way of the Bodhisattva:*

All that I possess and use
Is like the fleeting vision of a dream.
It fades into the realms of memory;
And fading, will be seen no more.

Whether we're conscious of it or not, the ground is always shifting. Nothing lasts, including us. There are probably very few people who, at any given time, are consumed with the idea "I'm going to die," but there is plenty of evidence that this thought, this fear, haunts us constantly. "I, too, am a brief and passing thing," observed Shantideva.

So what does it feel like to be human in this ambiguous, groundless state? For one thing, we grab at pleasure and try to avoid pain, but despite our efforts, we're always alternating between the two. Under the illusion that experiencing constant security and well-being is the ideal state, we do all sorts of things to try to achieve it: eat, drink, drug, work too hard, spend hours online or watching TV. But somehow we never quite achieve the state of unwavering satisfaction we're seeking. At times we feel good: physically nothing hurts and mentally all's well. Then it changes, and we're hit with physical pain or mental anguish. I imagine it would even be possible to chart how pleasure and pain alternate in our lives, hour by hour, day after day, year in and year out, first one and then the other predominating.

But it's not impermanence per se, or even knowing we're going to die, that is the cause of our suffering, the Buddha taught. Rather, it's our resistance to the fundamental uncertainty of our situation. Our discomfort arises from all of our efforts to put ground under our feet, to realize our dream of constant okayness. When we resist change, it's called suffering. But when we can completely let go and not struggle against it, when we can embrace the groundlessness of our situation and relax into its dynamic quality, that's called enlightenment, or awakening to our true nature, to our fundamental goodness. Another word for this is *freedom*—freedom from struggling against the fundamental ambiguity of being human.

What the fundamental ambiguity of being human points to is that as much as we want to, we can never say, "This is the only true way. This is how it is. End of discussion." In his interview, Chris Hedges also talked about the pain that ensues when a group or religion insists that its view is the one true view. As individuals we, too, have plenty of fundamentalist tendencies. We use them to comfort ourselves. We grab on to a position or belief as a way of neatly explaining reality, unwilling to tolerate the uncertainty and discomfort of staying open to other possibilities. We cling to that position as our personal platform and become very dogmatic about it.

The root of these fundamentalist tendencies, these dogmatic tendencies, is a fixed identity—a fixed view we have of ourselves as good or bad, worthy or unworthy, this or that. With a fixed identity, we have to busy ourselves with trying to rearrange reality, because reality doesn't always conform to our view.

When I first came to Gampo Abbey, I thought of myself as a likable, flexible, openhearted, open-minded person. Part of that was true, but there was another part that wasn't. For one thing, I was a terrible director. The other residents felt disempowered by me. They pointed out my shortcomings, but I couldn't hear what they were saying because my fixed identity was so strong. Every time new people came to live at the abbey, I got the same kind of negative feedback, but still I didn't hear it. This went on for a few years. Then one day, as if they had all gotten together and staged an intervention, I finally heard what everyone had been telling me about how my behavior was affecting them. At last, the message got through.

That's what it means to be in denial: you can't hear anything that doesn't fit into your fixed identity. Even something positive—you're kind or you did a great job or you have a wonderful sense of humor—is filtered through this fixed identity. You can't take it in unless it's already part of your self-definition.

In Buddhism we call the notion of a fixed identity "ego clinging." It's how we try to put solid ground under our feet in an ever-shifting world. Meditation practice starts to erode that fixed identity. As you sit, you begin to see yourself with more clarity, and you notice how attached you are to your opinions about yourself. Often the first blow to the fixed identity is precipitated by a crisis. When things start to fall apart in your life, as they did in mine when I came to Gampo Abbey, you feel as if your whole world is crumbling. But actually it's your fixed identity that's crumbling. And as Chögyam Trungpa used to tell us, that's cause for celebration.

The purpose of the spiritual path is to unmask, to take off our armor. When that happens, it feels like a crisis because it *is* a crisis—a fixed-identity crisis. The Buddha taught that the fixed identity is the cause of our suffering. Looking deeper, we could say that the real cause of suffering is not being able to tolerate uncertainty—and thinking that it's perfectly sane, perfectly normal, to deny the fundamental groundlessness of being human.

Ego clinging is our means of denial. Once we have the fixed idea "this is me," then we see everything as a threat or a promise—or something we couldn't care less about. Whatever we encounter, we're either attracted to it or averse to it or indifferent to it, depending on how much of a threat to our self-image it represents. The fixed identity is our false security. We maintain it by filtering all of our experience through this perspective. When we like someone, it's generally because they make us feel good. They don't blow our trip, don't disturb our fixed identity, so we're buddies. When we don't like someone—they're not on our wavelength, so we don't want to hang out with them—it's generally because they challenge our fixed identity. We're uncomfortable in their presence because they don't confirm us in the ways we want to be confirmed, so we can't function in the ways we want to function. Often we think of the people we don't like as our enemies, but in fact, they're all-important to us. They're our greatest teachers: special messengers who show up just when we need them, to point out our fixed identity.

The discomfort associated with groundlessness, with the fundamental ambiguity of being human, comes from our attachment to wanting things to be a certain way. The Tibetan word for attachment is *shenpa*. My teacher Dzigar Kongtrül calls shenpa the barometer of ego clinging, a gauge of our self-involvement and self-importance. Shenpa has a visceral quality associated with grasping or, conversely, pushing away. This is the feeling of *I like, I want, I need* and *I don't like, I don't want, I don't need, I want it to go away.* I think of shenpa as being hooked. It's that stuck feeling, that tightening or closing down or withdrawing we experience when we're uncomfortable with what's going on. Shenpa is also the urge to find relief from those feelings by clinging to something that gives us pleasure.

Anything can trigger our clinging, our attachments: someone criticizes our work or looks at us the wrong way; the dog chews our favorite shoes; we spill on our best tie. One minute we're feeling fine, then something happens, and suddenly we're hooked into anger, jealousy, blame, recrimination, or self-doubt. This discomfort, this sense of being triggered because things are not "right," because we want them to last longer or to go away, is the felt experience, the visceral experience of the fundamental ambiguity of being human.

For the most part, our attachment, our shenpa, arises involuntarily—our habitual response to feeling insecure. When we're hooked, we turn to anything to relieve the discomfort—food, alcohol, sex, shopping, being critical or unkind. But there is something more fruitful we can do when that edgy feeling arises. It's similar to the way we can deal with pain. One popular way of relating to physical pain is mindfulness meditation. It involves directing your full attention to the pain and breathing in and out of the spot that hurts. Instead of trying to avoid the discomfort, you open yourself completely to it. You become receptive to the painful sensation without dwelling on the story your mind has concocted: *It's bad; I shouldn't feel this way; maybe it will never go away.*

When you contact the all-worked-up feeling of shenpa, the basic instruction is the same as in dealing with physical pain. Whether it's a feeling of *I like* or *I don't like,* or an emotional state like loneliness, depression, or anxiety, you open yourself fully to the sensation, free of interpretation. If you've tried this approach with physical pain, you know that the result can be quite miraculous. When you give your full attention to your knee or your back or your head— whatever hurts—and drop the good/bad, right/wrong story line and simply experience the pain directly for even a short time, then your ideas about the pain, and often the pain itself, will dissolve.

Shantideva said that the suffering we experience with physical pain is entirely conceptual. It comes not from the sensation itself but from how we view it. He used the example of the Karna, a sect in ancient India in which the members burned and cut themselves as part of their ritual practice. They associated the extreme pain with spiritual ecstasy, so it had a positive meaning for them. Many athletes experience something similar when they "feel the burn." The physical sensation in itself is neither good nor bad; it's our interpretation of it that makes it so.

I'm reminded of something that happened when my daredevil son was about twelve years old. We were standing on a tiny platform on the prow of a large ship—kind of like Leonardo DiCaprio and Kate Winslet in the movie *Titanic*—and I started to describe to him my fear of heights. I told him I wasn't sure I could stay there, that I was having all sorts of physical sensations and my legs were turning to mush. I'll never forget the look on his face when he said, "Mom, that's exactly what *I* feel!" The difference is that he *loved* the feeling. All of my nieces and nephews are bungee jumpers and spelunkers and enjoy adventures that I avoid at any cost just because I have an aversion to the same feeling that gives them a thrill.

But there's an approach we can take to the fundamental ambiguity of being human that allows us to work with, rather than retreat from, feelings like fear and aversion. If we can get in touch with the sensation as sensation and open ourselves to it without labeling it good or bad, then even when we feel the urge to draw back, we can stay present and move forward into the feeling.

In *My Stroke of Insight*, the brain scientist Jill Bolte Taylor's book about her recovery from a massive stroke, she explains the physiological mechanism behind emotion: an emotion like anger that's an automatic response lasts just ninety seconds from the moment it's triggered until it runs its course. One and a half minutes, that's all. When it lasts any longer, which it usually does, it's because we've chosen to rekindle it.

The fact of the shifting, changing nature of our emotions is something we could take advantage of. But do we? No. Instead, when an emotion comes up, we fuel it with our thoughts, and what should last one and a half minutes may be drawn out for ten or twenty years. We just keep recycling the story line. We keep strengthening our old habits.

Most of us have physical or mental conditions that have caused us distress in the past. And when we get a whiff of one coming—an incipient asthma attack, a symptom of chronic fatigue, a twinge of anxiety—we panic. Instead of relaxing with the feeling and letting it do its minute and a half while we're fully open and receptive to it, we say, "Oh no, oh no, here it is again." We refuse to feel fundamental ambiguity when it comes in this form, so we do the thing that will be most detrimental to us: we rev up our thoughts about it. *What if this happens? What if that happens?* We stir up a lot of mental activity. Body, speech, and mind become engaged in running away from the feeling, which only keeps it going and going and going.

We can counter this response by training in being present. A woman who was familiar with Jill Bolte Taylor's observation about the duration of emotion sent me a letter describing what she does when an uneasy feeling comes up. "I just do the one-and-a-half-minute thing," she wrote.

So, that's a good practice instruction: When you contact groundlessness, one way to deal with that edgy, queasy feeling is to "do the one-and-a-half-minute thing."

Acknowledge the feeling, give it your full, compassionate, even welcoming attention, and even if it's only for a few seconds, drop the story line about the feeling. This allows you to have a direct experience of it, free of interpretation. Don't fuel it with concepts or opinions about whether it's good or bad. Just be present with the sensation. Where is it located in your body? Does it remain the same for very long? Does it shift and change?

Ego or *fixed identity* doesn't just mean we have a fixed idea about ourselves. It also means that we have a fixed idea about everything we perceive. I have a fixed idea about you; you have a fixed idea about me. And once there is that feeling of separation, it gives rise to strong emotions. In Buddhism, strong emotions like anger, craving, pride, and jealousy are known as *kleshas*—conflicting emotions that cloud the mind. The *kleshas* are our vehicle for escaping groundlessness, and therefore every time we give in to them, our preexisting habits are reinforced. In Buddhism, going around and around, recycling the same patterns, is called samsara. And samsara equals pain.

We keep trying to get away from the fundamental ambiguity of being human, and we can't. We can't escape it any more than we can escape change, any more than we can escape death. The cause of our suffering is our reaction to the reality of no escape: ego clinging and all the trouble that stems from it, all the things that make it difficult for us to be comfortable in our own skin and get along with one another.

If the way to deal with those feelings is to stay present

with them without fueling the story line, then it begs the question: *How* do we get in touch with the fundamental ambiguity of being human in the first place? In fact, it's not difficult, because underlying uneasiness is usually present in our lives. It's pretty easy to recognize but not so easy to interrupt. We may experience this uneasiness as anything from slight edginess to sheer terror. Anxiety makes us feel vulnerable, which we generally don't like. Vulnerability comes in many guises. We may feel off balance, as if we don't know what's going on, don't have a handle on things. We may feel lonely or depressed or angry. Most of us want to avoid emotions that make us feel vulnerable, so we'll do almost anything to get away from them.

But if, instead of thinking of these feelings as bad, we could think of them as road signs or barometers that tell us we're in touch with groundlessness, then we would see the feelings for what they really are: the gateway to liberation, an open doorway to freedom from suffering, the path to our deepest well-being and joy. We have a choice. We can spend our whole life suffering because we can't relax with how things really are, or we can relax and embrace the open-endedness of the human situation, which is fresh, unfixated, unbiased.

So the challenge is to notice the emotional tug of shenpa when it arises and to stay with it for one and a half minutes without the story line. Can you do this once a day, or many times throughout the day, as the feeling arises? This is the challenge. This is the process of unmasking, letting go, opening the mind and heart.

2

Life without the Story Line

MY GRANDDAUGHTER'S UNIVERSITY professor asked her students to leave their cell phones behind when they came to class. My granddaughter was amazed at how much more present and alert she was as a result. She observed that her whole generation was getting in-depth, intensive training in being distracted. To me, this underscores how important it is for her generation, and the generations that follow, and the generations that came before, to counter this trend by getting intensive training in staying present.

When you practice staying present, one thing you'll quickly discover is how persistent the story line is. Traditionally, in the Buddhist texts, our tendencies with their habitual story lines are described as seeds in the unconscious. When the right causes and conditions come together, these preexisting propensities pop up like flowers in the springtime. It's helpful to contemplate that it's these propensities and not what triggers them that are the real cause of our suffering.

I had a dream about my ex-husband: I was just settling down for a quiet evening at home when he arrived with six unknown guests and then disappeared, leaving me to take care of them. I was furious. When I woke up, I thought ruefully, "So much for being finished with anger: I guess the propensity is still there." Then I started thinking about an incident that had occurred the previous day, and I began to get furious all over again. This completely stopped me in my tracks, and I realized that waking or sleeping, it's just the same. It isn't the content of our movie that needs our attention, it's the projector. It isn't the current story line that's the root of our pain; it's our propensity to be bothered in the first place.

The propensity to feel sorry for ourselves, the propensity to be jealous, the propensity to get angry—our habitual, all-too-familiar emotional responses are like seeds that we just keep watering and nurturing. But every time we pause and stay present with the underlying energy, we stop reinforcing these propensities and begin to open ourselves to refreshingly new possibilities.

As you respond differently to an old habit, you may start to notice changes. In the past when you got angry, it might have taken you three days to cool down, but if you keep interrupting the angry thoughts, you may get to the point at which it takes only a day to drop the anger. Eventually, only hours or even one and a half minutes. You're starting to be liberated from suffering.

It's important to realize that interrupting thoughts isn't the same as repressing them. Repression is denial of what's happening, which only sends the thoughts underground where they can fester. At the same time, we don't want to keep chasing after the thoughts and getting hooked by them. Interrupting thoughts is somewhere between clinging to them and pushing them away. It's a way of allowing the thoughts to come and go, to arise and pass, to not be such a big deal.

The practice is to train in not following the thoughts, not in getting rid of thought altogether. That would be impossible. You may have thought-free moments and, as your meditation practice deepens, longer expanses of time that are thought free, but thoughts always come back. That's the nature of mind. You don't have to make thoughts the villain, however. You can just train in interrupting their momentum. The basic instruction is to let the thoughts go—or to label them "thinking"—and stay with the immediacy of your experience.

Everything in you will want to do the habitual thing, will want to pursue the story line. The story line is associated with certainty and comfort. It bolsters your very limited, static sense of self and holds out the promise of safety and happiness. But the promise is a false one; any happiness it brings is only temporary. The more you practice not escaping into the fantasy world of your thoughts and instead contacting the felt sense of groundlessness, the more accustomed you'll become to experiencing emotions as simply sensation—free of concept, free of story line, free of fixed ideas of bad and good.

Still, the tendency to scramble for security will try to reassert itself and gain some ground. We can't underestimate the very real (and very fleeting) comfort it provides. The meditation teacher Tara Brach, in her book *Radical Acceptance,* describes a practice she uses at such times. It's based on the Buddha's encounters with his nemesis, Mara, a demon who kept appearing to tempt the Buddha to give up his spiritual resolve and go back to his old unaware ways. Psychologically, Mara represents the false promise of happiness and security offered by our habitual responses. So whenever Mara appeared, often with beautiful women or other temptations in tow, the Buddha would say, "I see you, Mara. I know you're a trickster. I know what you're trying to do." And then he'd invite his nemesis to sit down for tea. When we're tempted to go back to our habitual ways of avoiding groundlessness, we can look temptation in the eye and say, "I see you, Mara," then sit down with the fundamental ambiguity of being human without any judgment of right or wrong.

In a book I read recently, the author talked about humans as transitional beings—beings who are neither fully caught nor fully free but are in the process of awakening. I find it helpful to think of myself this way. I'm in the process of becoming, in the process of evolving. I'm neither doomed nor completely free, but I'm creating my future with every word, every action, every thought. I find myself in a very dynamic situation with unimaginable potential. I have all the support I need to simply relax and be with the transitional, in-process quality of my life. I have all I need to engage in the process of awakening.

Rather than living a life of resistance and trying to disprove our basic situation of impermanence and change, we could contact the fundamental ambiguity and welcome it. We don't like to think of ourselves as fixed and unchanging, but emotionally we're very invested in it. We simply don't want the frightening, uneasy discomfort of feeling groundless. But we don't have to close down when we feel groundlessness in any form. Instead, we can turn toward it and say, "This is what freedom from fixed mind feels like. This is what freedom from closed-heartedness feels like. This is what unbiased, unfettered goodness feels like. Maybe I'll get curious and see if I can go beyond my resistance and experience the goodness."

Buddhism holds that the true nature of the mind is as vast as the sky and that thoughts and emotions are like clouds that, from our vantage point, obscure it. We're taught that if we want to experience the boundlessness of the sky, we'll need to get curious about those clouds. When we look deeply into the clouds, they fall apart, and there's the expanse of sky. It never went anywhere. It has always been here, momentarily hidden from us by the fleeting, shifting clouds.

The journey of awakening takes discipline and courage. Letting go of our cloud-like thoughts and emotions is by no means habitual at first. The thoughts and emotions may make it difficult for us to contact the openness of our minds, but they're like old friends who have accompanied us for as long as we can remember, and we're very resistant to saying good-bye. But each time you begin to meditate, you can decide that you're going to see if you can let the thoughts go and be right here with the immediacy of your experience. Perhaps you can be right here for only five seconds today, but any progress in the direction of nondistraction is positive.

Chögyam Trungpa had an image for our tendency to obscure the openness of our being; he called it "putting makeup on space." We can aspire to experience the space without the makeup. Staying open and receptive for even a short time starts to interrupt our deep-seated resistance to feeling what we're feeling, to staying present where we are.

Believing in the story line—identifying with the interpretations we put on our experience—is deeply ingrained in us. We assert our opinions as if they were indisputable: "Jane really is intrinsically horrible. I know this for a fact." "Ralph is intrinsically charming. There is absolutely no doubt about it." The way to weaken the habit of clinging to fixed ideas and contact the fluidity of thoughts and emotions is to shift your focus to a wider perspective. Instead of getting caught in the drama, see if you can feel the dynamic energy of the thoughts and emotions. See if you can experience the space around the thoughts: experience how they arise in space, dwell for a while, and then return into space. If you don't suppress the thoughts and emotions and don't run with them, then you find yourself in an interesting place. The place of not rejecting or justifying is right in the middle of nowhere. It is here that you can finally embrace what you're feeling. It is here that you can look out and see the sky.

As you're meditating, memories of something distressing that happened in the past may bubble up. It can be quite freeing to see all of that. But if you revisit the memory of something distressing over and over, rehashing what happened and obsessing on the story line, it becomes part of your static identity. You're just strengthening your propensity to experience yourself as the one who was wronged, as the victim. You're strengthening a preexisting propensity to blame others—your parents and anyone else—as the ones who wronged you. Continuing to recycle the old story line is a way of avoiding fundamental ambiguity. Emotions stay on and on when we fuel them with words. It's like pouring kerosene on an ember to make it blaze. Without the words, without the repetitive thoughts, the emotions don't last longer than one and a half minutes.

Our identity, which seems so reliable, so substantial, is in fact very fluid, very dynamic. There are unlimited possibilities to what we might think, what we might feel, and how we might experience reality. We have what it takes to free ourselves from the suffering of a fixed identity and connect with the fundamental slipperiness and mystery of our being, which has no fixed identity. Your sense of yourself—who you think you are at the relative level—is a very restricted version of who you truly are. But the good news is that you can use your direct experience—who you seem to be at this very moment—as the doorway to your true nature. By fully touching this relative moment of time—the sound you're hearing, the smell you're smelling, the pain or comfort you're feeling right now—by being fully present to your experience, you contact the unlimited openness of your being.

All of our habitual patterns are efforts to maintain a predictable identity: "I am an angry person"; "I am a friendly person"; "I am a lowly worm." We can work with these mental habits when they arise and stay with our experience not just when we're meditating but also in daily life. Whether we're alone or with others, no matter what we're doing, uneasiness can float to the surface at any time. We may think those poignant, piercing feelings are signs of danger, but in fact, they're signals that we've just contacted the fundamental fluidity of life. Rather than hiding from these feelings by staying in the bubble of ego, we can let the truth of how things really are get through. These moments are great opportunities. Even if we're surrounded by people—in a business meeting, say—when we feel uncertainty arising, we can just breathe and be present with the feelings. We don't have to panic or withdraw into ourselves. There's no need to respond habitually. No need to fight or flee. We can stay engaged with others and at the same time acknowledge what we're feeling.

The instructions, in their simplest form, have three basic steps:

Be fully present.
Feel your heart.
And engage the next moment without an agenda.

I work with this method on the spot, right in the middle of things. The more I stay present in formal meditation, the more familiar this process becomes, and the easier it is to do it in the midst of everyday situations. But regardless of where we practice staying present, it will put us in touch with the uncertainty and change that are inherent in being alive. It will give us the chance to train in staying awake to, and present with, all that we've previously run from.

The Three Commitments are three levels of working with groundlessness. Underlying them all is the basic instruction to make friends with yourself—to be honest with yourself and kind. This begins with the willingness to stay present whenever you experience uneasiness. As these feelings arise, rather than running away, you lean into them. Instead of trying to get rid of thoughts and feelings, you become curious about them. As you become accustomed to experiencing sensation free of interpretation, you will come to understand that contacting the fundamental ambiguity of being human provides a precious opportunity—the opportunity to be with life just as it is, the opportunity to experience the freedom of life without a story line.

The First Commitment
Committing to Not Cause Harm

It is wonderful that human beings are willing to let
go of even their smallest corners of secrecy and privacy,
so that their holding on to anything is gone completely.
That is very brave.

—CHÖGYAM TRUNGPA RINPOCHE

3

Laying the Foundation

TOGETHER, THE THREE COMMITMENTS support us in relaxing with the fundamental dynamic quality of our lives. But what does it mean to live by commitment? This is an interesting question.

As the dictionary defines it, a commitment is a pledge, something that binds us emotionally and mentally to someone or something or a course of action. The way Tibetan Buddhism traditionally views it, living by commitment means more than simply acting or not acting. When we make a commitment, we set our intention clearly and know what we're vowing to do or not do. This is why it's so powerful. Chögyam Trungpa said that a vow to not kill, for example, has more power than just not killing. If a lion or tiger doesn't kill, that's virtuous, but when causes and conditions come together, the lion or tiger will almost certainly kill because that's its nature. For us, however, taking a vow—making a commitment—allows us to not act reflexively when we have an urge. We think twice before speaking or acting.

Commitment is at the very heart of freeing ourselves from old habits and fears. If we embark on the journey of doing this, it only makes sense to begin by laying a solid foundation. We can do this by working with the first commitment, the commitment to not cause harm. This is traditionally called the Pratimoksha Vow, or vow of personal liberation—liberation from the suffering that comes with resisting the reality of our situation, the fundamental groundlessness of life. Once, when Chögyam Trungpa was teaching about personal liberation, he described the first commitment as "saving yourself from samsaric neurosis." From the suffering of everyday life, in other words. As Khandro Rinpoche, another Tibetan Buddhist teacher, explains it, this commitment protects us from falling into or chasing after unnecessary cravings, unnecessary aggression, and unnecessary indifference. It's the foundation of the other two commitments—the vow to help others and the vow to embrace the world just as it is—and opens the doorway to relaxing joyfully with fluidity and change.

So how does the first commitment work? It involves working with your mind, your thoughts, and your emotions in order to notice and clearly acknowledge when you're trying to escape the fundamental uncertainty of life. What are you doing just to fill up time and space, to avoid being present? How are you acting in habitual ways? The first commitment supports us in not escaping into our old patterns—in seeing very clearly that we're about to exit, then making a conscious decision not to do it.

We all have our familiar exits: zoning out in front of the TV, compulsively checking e-mail, coming home at night and having three or four or six drinks, overeating, overworking. Sometimes our exit is just chatter, chatter, chatter—aimless chatter. Speech is a big part of what this commitment works with. There are endless ways we use our speech to distract ourselves. And not just talking aloud. Mentally we're engaged in almost constant conversation with ourselves. One of the reasons I appreciate meditation retreats is that I can get a really close look at how even in total silence I still keep myself busy with my mind.

The first commitment is about refraining from speech and actions that are harmful to ourselves and others. It liberates us by making us far more aware of what we're feeling, so that whenever the urge to lie or slander or take something that isn't given to us comes up—whenever we have the urge to act out our desires or aggression, or escape in any form—we refrain.

As a support in refraining from harmful speech and actions, it can be really helpful to commit to four traditional precepts, or directives: the precepts to not kill, to not steal, to not lie, and to not harm others with our sexual activity. We can commit to these precepts for one day or one week or a lifetime. There are hundreds of rules for fully ordained monks and nuns, but the Buddha said that the most important were these four. Basically, following the precepts gives us space to examine every nuance of the urge to express ourselves negatively and then, while fully acknowledging our feelings, make the choice to not do anything that would cause harm.

In its simplest terms, then, the path of liberation begins with refraining from hurting ourselves and others. When many people hear "refrain," they automatically think "repression" and assume that when an urge comes up, they should just push it under. In therapeutic circles, there's an ongoing debate about which causes more harm: repression or acting out. To me, they're equally harmful. Once you speak or act, there's a chain reaction, and other people's emotions become involved. Every time you speak or act out of aggression or craving or jealousy or envy or pride, it's like dropping a pebble into a pool of water and watching the ripples fan out; everyone around you is affected. Similarly, if you repress your feelings, everyone is affected by that too, because you're walking around like a keg of dynamite that's about to go off.

Refraining from speaking or acting out slows us down and enables us to see our habitual responses very, very clearly. Until we can see our reactions, we can never know precisely what causes us to stay stuck and what will help us to get free. It's important, however, to refrain in a spirit of *compassionate* self-reflection. We look at what we say and do based on a genuine trust in our basic goodness. We trust that we're fundamentally openhearted and open-minded and that when we're not confounded by our emotions, we know what will help and what will hurt.

When you come from the view that you're fundamentally good rather than fundamentally flawed, as you see yourself speak or act out, as you see yourself repress, you will have a growing understanding that you're not a bad person who needs to shape up but a good person with temporary, malleable habits that are causing you a lot of suffering. And then, in that spirit, you can become very familiar with these temporary but strongly embedded habits. You can see them so clearly and so compassionately that you don't continue to strengthen them.

The process of seeing your habits clearly is sometimes compared to having a big, blank canvas, then taking a paintbrush and making a dot on it. The empty canvas represents basic goodness, your basic unfettered nature; the dot represents a habit. It can be a very small dot, but against the empty canvas it really stands out. From this perspective, you can see very clearly whether you spoke or acted, or didn't speak or didn't act. So you can begin to train in knowing what you're doing when you're doing it—and in being kind to yourself about your speech and actions. You rejoice when you're able to acknowledge that you're caught in an old pattern and when you catch yourself before you speak or act out. We all carry around trunk loads of old habits, but very fortunately for us, they're removable. They don't have to weigh us down permanently. Refraining is very powerful because it gives us an opportunity to acknowledge when we're caught and then to get unstuck.

Each time we *don't* refrain but speak or act out instead, we're strengthening old habits, strengthening the *kleshas,* and strengthening the fixed sense of self. We're keeping the whole mechanism of suffering going. But when we refrain, we're allowing ourselves to feel the underlying uncertainty—that edgy, restless energy—without trying to escape. The escape routes are there, but we're not using them. We're getting in touch with the feeling of fundamental uneasiness and relaxing with it rather than being run around by our thoughts and emotions. We're not trying to eradicate thoughts; we're just training ourselves not to be so enmeshed in them. Dzigar Kongtrül has a sign on the front door of his retreat cabin that reads, "Don't believe everything you think." That's the basic idea here.

As we become more conscious of our thoughts and emotions and look at them with kindhearted interest and curiosity, we begin to see how we armor ourselves against pain. And we see how that armor also cuts us off from the pain—and the beauty—of other people. But as we let go of our repetitive stories and fixed ideas about ourselves—particularly deep-seated feelings of "I'm not okay"—the armor starts to fall apart, and we open into the spaciousness of our true nature, into who we really are beyond our transitory thoughts and emotions. We see that our armor is made up of nothing more than habits and fears, and we begin to feel that we can let those go.

The first commitment works with the causes of suffering and brings about the cessation of suffering by allowing us to see clearly what our escape routes are and enabling us not to take them. Science is demonstrating that every time we refrain but don't repress, new neural pathways open up in the brain. In not taking the old escape routes, we're predisposing ourselves to a new way of seeing ourselves, a new way of relating to the mysteriously unpredictable world in which we live.

The Three Commitments aren't moralistic—they have nothing to do with being a "good girl" or a "good boy." They're about opening ourselves to a vaster perspective and changing at the core. Understanding the first commitment and the basic premise of acknowledging our escape routes and not following them is the necessary foundation for understanding the succeeding commitments.

The first commitment is often called the narrow way because it's comparable to walking down a very narrow corridor. If you lose your awareness, you'll veer off course and bump into the wall, so you have to keep bringing your attention back to the path and walking straight ahead. At bottom, the commitment is very simple: we're either speaking or acting in order to escape, or we're not. The further commitments are more flexible and don't have such clear—and comforting—boundaries. So it's important to begin with this very straightforward approach: we don't speak or act out. Period. The first commitment requires us to be diligent about interrupting the momentum of habit, the momentum of running away. Otherwise, as the commitments become more challenging and more groundless, the moment we get a whiff of anxiety or uneasiness or dissatisfaction, we'll automatically exit.

Many of our escapes are involuntary: addiction and dissociating from painful feelings are two examples. Anyone who has worked with a strong addiction—compulsive eating, compulsive sex, abuse of substances, explosive anger, or any other behavior that's out of control—knows that when the urge comes on it's irresistible. The seduction is too strong. So we train again and again in less highly charged situations in which the urge is present but not so overwhelming. By training with everyday irritations, we develop the knack of refraining when the going gets rough. It takes patience and an understanding of how we're hurting ourselves not to continue taking the same old escape route of speaking or acting out.

I often hear people say, "Oh, I don't need to make a commitment not to kill. I don't kill anyway." Or "I don't steal, and I'm not a monk or a nun, but I've been celibate for twenty years, so what's the point of committing to the precept against harmful sexual relations?" The point in keeping the precepts is that you're getting at something deeper. At the level of everyday behavior, refraining from killing, lying, stealing, or harming others with your sexual activity is called outer renunciation, a sort of keeping to the list. On an outer level, you follow the rules. But outer renunciation puts you in touch with what's happening *inside:* the clinging and fixating, the tendency to avoid the underlying queasy-feeling groundlessness. Refraining from harmful speech and action is outer renunciation; choosing not to escape the underlying feelings is inner renunciation. The precepts are a device to put us in touch with the underlying uneasiness, the fundamental dynamic quality of being alive. Working with this feeling and the neurosis it triggers is inner renunciation.

If I make a commitment to not slander or gossip or use harsh speech, but I'm living by myself in a cabin in the woods with no one to talk to, then it's easy to keep the precept against harmful speech. But if the second I'm with other people, I start gossiping, then I didn't learn much about the damaging effect of engaging in hurtful words. And I didn't learn much about the emotions that are motivating my gossip. Keeping the precept, however, means I'll think twice before engaging in that conversation. So, whether we commit to four precepts, five precepts, eight precepts, or hundreds of precepts, having made the commitment protects us when temptation comes.

As a practice, you can make a commitment to keep one or more of the precepts for one day a week or twice a month or the duration of a meditation retreat or a lifetime. The first four precepts are considered the most basic. The fifth, on refraining from drugs and alcohol, is often taken along with the other four. The wording of the five precepts as set out below is loosely based on a version by the Vietnamese Zen master Thich Nhat Hanh.

1. ON PROTECTING LIFE

Aware of the suffering brought about by the destruction of life, I vow to not kill any living being. I will do my best to cultivate nonaggression and compassion and to learn to protect life.

2. ON RESPECTING WHAT BELONGS TO OTHERS

Aware of the suffering caused by stealing or taking anything that belongs to others, I vow to not take what is not offered. I will do my best to respect the property of others.

3. On Not Harming Others with Our Sexual Energy

Aware of the suffering caused by unmindful or aggressive sexual energy, I vow to be faithful to my current partner and not harm others with my sexual energy. I will do my best to be aware of what harms myself and others and to nurture true love and respect, free from attachment. I aspire to serve and protect all beings.

4. On Mindful Speech

Aware of the suffering caused by unmindful speech, I vow to cultivate right speech. Knowing that words can create happiness or suffering, I will do my best to not lie, to not gossip or slander, to not use harsh or idle speech, and to not say things that bring about division or hatred. I aspire always to speak the truth.

5. On Protecting the Body and Mind

Aware of the suffering caused by alcohol, drugs, and other intoxicants, I vow to not drink liquor or use drugs. I will do my best to live my life in a way that will increase my inner strength and flexibility as well as my openness to all beings and to life itself.

It's not enough, however, just to follow the rules—follow the precepts to the letter. Sticking to the outer form can be just another way of strengthening my fixed identity, a way of shoring up my self-image as a virtuous person, as someone who's purer than others. In other words, it may only strengthen pride. Unless I also include inner renunciation and admit to the ways I'm propping myself up by building this virtuous identity, then simply following the rules can be almost as damaging as breaking them.

In *The Way of the Bodhisattva,* Shantideva lists all the ways he can think of to express being on the verge of speaking or acting neurotically. And in every case, he advises us not to do it. When feelings of desire or craving arise, or the urge to speak or act out of aggression arises, "Do not act!" he warns. "Be silent, do not speak!" That's the basic instruction of the first commitment: *Don't act, don't speak.* That's the outer work. And then there's also the inner work of exploring what happens next when you don't act and don't speak. Shantideva's advice is:

> When the mind is wild with mockery
> And filled with pride and haughty arrogance,
> And when you want to show the hidden faults of others,
> To bring up old dissensions or to act deceitfully,
> And when you want to fish for praise
> Or criticize and spoil another's name
> Or use harsh language, sparring for a fight,
> It's then that like a log you should remain.

If there's no temptation to act out, then the commitment to not harm won't be as transformative as when we want to speak or act out—when we yearn for wealth, attention, fame, honors, recognition, and "a circle of admirers," as Shantideva puts it—but we don't follow through on our desire. Maybe you want everyone to like you. Or you want to put someone down and cultivate advantage for yourself. Or you want to gossip. Or you're impatient. Or you're "sparring for a fight." Maybe you're tempted to engage in what Shantideva calls "haughty speech and insolence" or in cynicism, sarcasm, or condescension. If you acknowledge what's happening and refrain from acting, that opens up some space in your mind. Clinging to views and opinions, thinking you're always right and lording it over others, keeps you endlessly stuck. You continue to make people feel angry or inferior and keep landing in unnecessary battles. What's the remedy? Examine yourself, Shantideva tells us. See exactly what you're doing. "Note harmful thoughts and every futile striving," he says. "Apply the remedies to keep a steady mind."

When you're refraining—when you're feeling the pull of habitual thoughts and emotions but you're not escaping by acting or speaking out—you can try this inner renunciation exercise:

Notice how you feel: What does it feel like in the body to have these cravings or aggressive urges?

Notice your thinking: What sort of thoughts do these feelings give birth to?

Notice your actions: How do you treat yourself and other people when you feel this way?

This is what living by commitment means. Once when Chögyam Trungpa was asked, "Commitment to what?" he replied, "Commitment to sanity." We could also say commitment to courage, commitment to developing unconditional friendship with yourself.

To further get at what inner renunciation means, you could try the following practice of *renouncing one thing*:

For one day (or one day a week), refrain from something you habitually do to run away, to escape. Pick something concrete, such as overeating or excessive sleeping or overworking or spending too much time texting or checking e-mails. Make a commitment to yourself to gently and compassionately work with refraining from this habit for this one day. Really commit to it. Do this with the intention that it will put you in touch with the underlying anxiety or uncertainty that you've been avoiding. Do it and see what you discover.

When you refrain from habitual thoughts and behavior, the uncomfortable feelings will still be there. They don't magically disappear. Over the years, I've come to call resting with the discomfort "the detox period," because when you don't act on your habitual reactions, it's like giving up an addiction. You're left with the feelings you were trying to escape. The practice is to make a wholehearted relationship with that.

The underlying anxiety can be very strong. You may experience it as hopelessness or even terror. But the basic view is that if you can remain with the feeling, if you can go through the fear, the hopelessness, the resistance in its various forms, you will find basic goodness. Everything opens up. A poem by the late Rick Fields speaks to this process:

This world—absolutely pure
As is. Behind the fear,
Vulnerability. Behind that,
Sadness, then compassion
And behind that the vast sky.

With this practice, this exploration of inner renunciation, we can gradually see beyond our fear-based fixed identity. When we make a compassionate, fearless relationship with the reality of the human condition—with our habits, our emotions, with groundlessness—then gradually something shifts fundamentally, and we experience the sky-like, unbiased nature of our mind. Chögyam Trungpa said that this state of mind is completely fresh, completely new, completely unbiased, and we call it enlightenment. In other words, enlightenment is already here; we just need to touch it and know it and trust it. But first we make a journey through our resistance, knowing its every nuance, its strategies and exits. In this way we uncover that awareness.

But what happens if we break this commitment? What happens, for instance, when we act or speak in a harmful way? What do we do then? If falling into habitual patterns, habitual escapes, is inevitable from time to time, how do we return to the path?

There's a practice in Buddhism called Sojong that gives us an opportunity to reflect on where we are in terms of refraining and, when we feel that we've really made a mess of things, to put that behind us and start anew. Traditionally, Sojong takes place twice a month, on the full and new moon days. The day before, each person reviews the preceding two weeks and reflects: *What have I done with my body? What have I done with my speech? What about my mind: is it steady or all over the place and never present?* As much as possible, we explore these questions without self-criticism or blame. At Gampo Abbey, on the day before Sojong, we come together and talk about what we've been working with over the past two weeks. We share our insights about what helps and what hinders.

Sojong itself is a little like the fourth and fifth steps in a Twelve Step program, which call for making "a searching and fearless" self-inventory, recognizing where we've gone off course, then sharing this with another person. Sojong is a kind of antiguilt process that allows us to assess ourselves honestly, acknowledge what we've done and where we are, then let go of self-judgment and move on. Instead of holding on to the view, "I'm hopeless. Week after week, month after month, year after year go by, and I can never stop lying" (or whatever your habit is), you can say, "Well, this is where I am now. I fully declare what's happened now and in the past, and I go forward with a sense of a fresh start."

You don't have to say this aloud to a group or another person, but most people find it easier to let go of self-judgment if they share their observations with someone else—a friend, perhaps, or a spiritual advisor. However you do it, the aim is to be fully honest and, at the same time, to shed feelings of guilt. One time, a group of students were asking Chögyam Trungpa about guilt. Among them was a man who had killed people in the Vietnam War and was tortured by self-loathing and guilt. Chögyam Trungpa told him, "That was then. This is now. You can always connect with your true nature at any time and be free of everything that went before." Instead of letting our regrets drag us down, we can use them to spur us on to not repeat harmful acts but to learn from them how to be wiser in the future. We are fundamentally good, not fundamentally flawed, and we can trust this.

It's never too late to restore your vow, to renew your commitment to refrain. But at the same time, if you're not fully aware and conscious of what you're doing, then the patterns will just become stronger and stronger, and you'll continue to do the same things over and over again. So the process that begins with the first commitment is an opportunity to gain clarity about your mind and speech and actions and, at the same time, acknowledge honestly and gently what has happened in the past, then lay your harmful deeds aside and go forward.

Nobody's perfect in keeping the commitment to not harm. But still, students often ask me, "How can I make this vow with any integrity? If I'm going to break it at all, then what's the point?" Patrul Rinpoche, a Buddhist master who lived in the eighteenth century, basically said there is no way to escape harming. He devotes an entire section of his book *The Words of My Perfect Teacher* to all the ways we cause harm: countless beings suffer from making the clothes we wear, from bringing us the food we eat. Beings suffer even when we walk. "Who is not guilty of having crushed countless tiny insects underfoot?" he asks. Our situation is inescapable because of our interconnectedness with all things. What makes the difference is our intention to not harm. On an everyday level, the intention to not harm means using our body, our speech, and our mind in such a way that we don't knowingly hurt people, animals, birds, insects—any being—with our actions or words.

And we not only vow to not harm, Patrul Rinpoche says, we also commit to doing the opposite: We help. We heal. We do everything we can to benefit others.

4

Be Fully Present,
Feel Your Heart, and Leap

THE ON-THE-SPOT practice of *being fully present, feeling your heart, and greeting the next moment with an open mind* can be done at any time: when you wake up in the morning, before a difficult conversation, whenever fear or discomfort arises. This practice is a beautiful way to claim your warriorship, your spiritual warriorship. In other words, it is a way to claim your courage, your kindness, your strength. Whenever it occurs to you, you can pause briefly, touch in with how you're feeling both physically and mentally, and then connect with your heart—even putting your hand on your heart, if you want to. This is a way of extending warmth and acceptance to whatever is going on for you right now. You might have an aching back, an upset stomach, panic, rage, impatience, calmness, joy— whatever it is, you can let it be there just as it is, without labeling it good or bad, without telling yourself you should or shouldn't be feeling that way. Having connected with what is, with love and acceptance, you can go forward with curiosity and courage. I call this third step "taking a leap."

In order to do this practice, most of us need a bit of support. It's not always easy to be fully present—or even partly present. It's not always easy to extend warmth to ourselves. It's even less easy to let go of our habitual ways of being in the world and take a leap. Fortunately, meditation provides us with exactly the support we need. It's a practice for staying present, for nurturing our heart, and for letting go.

Just as we might practice the piano to cultivate our musical ability or practice a sport to cultivate our athletic ability, we can practice meditation to nurture the natural ability of the mind to be present, to feel loving-kindness, to open beyond fixed opinions and views. The meditation that I was taught and that I practice has three main parts: posture, the object of meditation, and the way we relate to thoughts. As I go through these instructions, I'll point out the aspects that pertain to staying present, feeling your heart, and letting go.

The basic instruction starts with posture—with the way our body supports us while we're meditating. We begin by being fully present in our body with awareness of our seat, our legs, our arms, our torso. We take a noble, upright but relaxed posture, which helps us settle internally and contact a feeling of confidence and dignity within ourselves. We are claiming our warriorship, claiming our bravery, claiming a fundamental feeling of all-rightness. If the body is uplifted, the mind will be uplifted. The six points of good posture taught by Chögyam Trungpa help us in this process. They are the seat, the legs, the torso, the hands, the eyes, and the mouth.

The first point is *the seat*. Sometimes meditation is referred to as taking your seat. Taking your seat means sitting in meditation with the confidence that you have the right to be there, the right to be fully awake. Literally speaking, the seat should be flat and well balanced. If you prefer, you can sit with a meditation cushion tucked under your buttocks to lift your pelvis and tilt it slightly forward; this helps you sit comfortably without slumping. Whichever way you sit, your body should be in alignment—leaning neither too far forward nor too far backward nor to the right or left. The idea is to find a comfortable position so that you won't wiggle or keep changing position during your meditation period.

If you find sitting on a cushion uncomfortable, you can sit in a chair, preferably one with a straight back and a flat seat. Sit slightly forward on the seat so that you're not leaning against the back of the chair and place both feet flat on the floor.

The second point of good posture concerns *the legs*. If you're sitting on a cushion, your legs should be folded comfortably in front of you. To reduce strain on your back, it's best to make sure that your knees are not higher than your hips. You can experiment with different leg positions until your find one that is comfortable. If, while you're meditating, you become very uncomfortable, you can temporarily assume the resting posture: keeping your back straight, bend your knees and draw your legs up toward your chest. You can wrap your arms around your legs to keep them steady.

The next point of good posture is *the torso* (your body from the neck to the seat). Whatever posture you choose, the idea is to keep the torso upright. Chögyam Trungpa's instruction was "open front, strong back." Strong back doesn't mean a rigid back but rather an erect spine and shoulders that aren't hunched. This leaves the heart area wide open and allows you to feel your heart. If you begin to slump, the heart area becomes constricted, as if you were closing your heart. So you sit upright again and open, ready to welcome whatever arises. Some people keep the torso upright by visualizing the vertebrae stacked one on top of the other. Others imagine an invisible cord attached to the crown of the head, pulling the body upward. The chin should be tucked slightly, not jutting forward.

The hands are the fourth point of good posture. One classic position is to place your hands on your thighs, palms down. Traditionally, this is called the "resting the mind" position. Arm lengths vary, so you will need to experiment to see where on your thighs you can comfortably rest your hands so that your body stays in alignment.

Then we come to *the eyes*, the fifth point of good posture. Some people like to meditate with their eyes closed, but in the tradition I trained in, we keep the eyes open, gazing softly downward about four to six feet in front of us. Keeping the eyes open is a way of cultivating open receptivity—open receptivity to whatever thoughts and emotions arise in the mind during meditation, open receptivity to the immediate environment. This aids us in being fully present and cultivating an attitude of acceptance.

The final point of posture is *the mouth*. The mouth stays open very slightly. The purpose of this is to allow the jaw to relax and to let the breath pass easily through both the nose and the mouth.

When we first sit down to meditate, we begin by running through the six points of good posture, checking each one in turn. This is sometimes called "flashing back to the sense of being." It allows us to be present in our body as we watch the movie of life unfold.

We can practice being present throughout the day: we don't have to be meditating formally. The object or focus of mindfulness can be anything that brings us back to right where we are. If we're out walking, the object of meditation could be the motion of our legs and feet. If we're washing dishes, it could be our hands. We can bring mindfulness to anything—opening a door, washing our hair, making the bed.

The object or focus of formal meditation is the breath. Being mindful of the breath keeps us present. When we become distracted, as we probably will, we don't make it a big deal. Our attitude toward the practice is always one of warmth and acceptance. As my teacher Sakyong Mipham often says, we should meditate from our heart. When the mind wanders, we simply bring it back to the present, over and over again. We don't try to breathe in some contrived way but let the breath flow in and out naturally. By its very nature, the breath is not graspable; there is nothing at all to hold on to. Our breath, therefore, provides an immediate connection with impermanence as we experience it continually arising and dissolving back into space. Using the breath as the object of meditation introduces us to the fundamental groundlessness of life and to the experience of letting go. This provides training in the third step of the three-step practice, taking a leap. Because meditation is a training in being open to and relaxed with whatever arises, it also gives us the proper foundation for self-acceptance and warmth toward others. In other words, it gives us practice in feeling our heart.

Without straining, we rest our attention lightly on the breath as it goes in and out. Some people prefer to focus only on the out breath. Either way, the attention should be so light that only one-quarter of our awareness is on the breath, while three-quarters is on the space around the breath. The breath goes out and dissolves into space, then we breathe in again. This continues without any need to make it happen or to control it. Each time the breath goes out, we simply let it go. Whatever occurs—our thoughts or emotions, sounds or movement in the environment—we train in accepting it without any value judgments.

Using the breath as the object of meditation supports the mind's natural capacity to be present. But the first thing most of us notice when we start meditating is how easily our mind wanders, how easily we're distracted and become lost in planning and remembering. When the mind wanders, the breath serves as a home base we can always return to.

The habit of exiting, of escaping into thoughts and daydreams, is a common occurrence. In fact, fantasy is where we spend most of our time. The Zen teacher Charlotte Joko Beck called these flights of fancy "the substitute life."

Of course, we don't have to be meditating for the mind to wander off to this substitute life. We can be listening to someone talking and mentally just depart. The person is right in front of us, but we're on the beach at Waikiki. The main way we depart is by keeping up a running internal commentary on what's going on and what we're feeling: *I like this, I don't like that, I'm hot, I'm cold,* and so on. In fact, we can become so caught up in this internal dialogue that the people around us become invisible. An important part of meditation practice, therefore, is to nonaggressively drop that ongoing conversation in our head and joyfully come back to the present, being present in the body, being present in the mind, not envisioning the future or reliving the past but, if only briefly, showing up for this very moment.

To bring our attention back to the breath, we use a technique called labeling. Whenever we notice that we're distracted, we make a mental note, "thinking," then gently return our attention to the breath. It's important to have a kind attitude as we meditate, to train in making friends with ourselves rather than strengthening rigidity and self-criticism. Therefore, we try to label with a good-hearted, nonjudgmental mind. I like to imagine that thoughts are bubbles and that labeling them is like touching a bubble with a feather. That's very different from attacking thoughts as if they were clay pigeons we were trying to shoot down.

One student said that he called the voice in his head "the little sergeant." The sergeant was always harsh and critical, always barking orders: "Shape up! Do it the right way!" Instead, we cultivate unconditional self-acceptance. We cultivate feeling the heart. When we find that we're labeling thinking in harsh tones, we can stop and use a kinder voice.

There's a traditional form of meditation that involves very closely observing the kinds of thoughts that are arising and labeling them accordingly—harsh thought, entertainment thought, passion thought, angry thought, and so on. But since there is judgment involved in labeling thoughts in this way, Chögyam Trungpa taught instead to drop all labels that characterize thoughts as virtuous or unvirtuous and simply label thoughts "thinking." That's just what it is, thinking—no more, no less.

Shantideva enthusiastically urges us to stay present even with extreme discomfort. "There is nothing that does not grow light, through habit and familiarity," he says. "Putting up with little cares, I'll train myself to bear with great adversity."

But how, exactly, do we train in being present not just for the "little cares"—the minor annoyances of life—but also for "great adversity"? The Tibetan Buddhist master Dzongsar Khyentse called the irritations of daily life "bourgeois suffering." It is by opening fully to these everyday inconveniences—our favorite restaurant's being closed, being stuck in traffic, bad weather, hunger pangs—that we develop the capacity to stay present in the face of greater challenges. The practice of meditation gives us a way of working with thoughts and emotions, with the fears and doubts that arise over and over again in our minds when they are triggered by difficult outer circumstances. Supported by the breath, we learn to stay present with all of our experience, even great adversity, and to label the thoughts, let them go, and come back to the here and now.

Some people think that labeling is cumbersome and unnecessary, but the practice can be very profound. Labeling without judgment helps us to see the very nature of thoughts as ephemeral, always dissolving, always elusive, never predictable. When we say "thinking," we are pointing to the empty nature of thoughts, to the transparency of thoughts and emotions.

This basic meditation technique is designed to help us remain open and receptive not only to our thoughts and emotions, not only to outer circumstances and the people we encounter, but also to groundlessness itself, to this underlying energy that is so threatening to the part of us that wants certainty. This practice allows us to get very close to this edgy, uncomfortable energy. It allows us to become familiar with nothing to hold on to, with stepping into the next moment without knowing what will happen. It gives us practice in taking a leap. It also gives us the space to notice how the mind immediately tries to entertain us or come up with scenarios of escape or revenge or do whatever else it does to try to provide security and comfort.

As we continue the practice, we will come to experience life's impermanent and changing energy not just as threatening but also as refreshing, liberating, and inspiring. It's the same energy—we just experience it in two different ways. Either we can relax into it, seeing it as the true nature of our mind, our unconditional goodness, or we can react against it. When we react against it—when we feel the energy as scary and uncomfortable and restless, and our body wants to move and our mind wants to latch on to something—we can train in the basic technique of labeling thoughts and letting them go, then bringing our attention back to the breath and staying present with the feeling. If for only ten minutes a day, we can sit and practice being mindful, being awake, being right here. We can practice warmth and acceptance. We can train in letting go of the breath, letting go of the thoughts, and greeting the next moment with an open mind. This is the preparation we need for the three-step practice, not to mention for living a wakeful life.

Sakyong Mipham recommends that as we sit down to meditate, we contemplate our intention for the session. Our intention might be to strengthen the natural stability of mind by training in continually coming back to the body, to our mood right now, and to our environment. Or our intention might be to make friends with ourselves, to be less stern and judgmental as we meditate, so we might train in noticing our tone of voice when we label and lightening up and not being too tight or goal oriented in our practice. Our intention might be to let go and not hold the breath tightly as if it were a life raft, not cling to our thoughts, not believe our story lines. We might intend to acknowledge thoughts as they arise and train in letting them go. Our intention might be to train in all of these—or in something different altogether, something that is particularly important to us.

Each day, we can set aside time for meditation. It can be as short as five or ten minutes or as long as we want to keep going.

––––––––––––––––––––

First, contemplate your intention for this practice session. Then run through the six points of good posture to settle your body. If you like, you can then count breaths from 1 to 10, or from 1 to 20, to settle the mind. Then drop the counting and simply bring light awareness to the breath. As you continue to meditate, maintain gentle awareness of the breath as it comes in and goes out, or just as it goes out. When the mind wanders, gently label the thoughts "thinking" and joyfully, without judgment, bring your attention back to the breath.

––––––––––––––––––––

Over time, as the thinking mind begins to settle, we'll start to see our patterns and habits far more clearly. This can be a painful experience. I can't overestimate the importance of accepting ourselves exactly as we are right now, not as we wish we were or think we ought to be. By cultivating nonjudgmental openness to ourselves and to whatever arises, to our surprise and delight we will find ourselves genuinely welcoming the never-pin-downable quality of life, experiencing it as a friend, a teacher, and a support, and no longer as an enemy.

5

Staying in the Middle

A MEAN WORD or a snide remark, a disdainful or disapproving facial expression, aggressive body language—these are all ways that we can cause harm. The first commitment allows us to slow down enough to become very intimate with how we feel when we're pushed to the limit, very intimate with the urge to strike out or withdraw, become a bully or go numb. We become very mindful of the feeling of craving, the feeling of aversion, the feeling of wanting to speak or act out.

Not acting on our habitual patterns is only the first step toward not harming others or ourselves. The transformative process begins at a deeper level when we contact the rawness we're left with whenever we refrain. As a way of working with our aggressive tendencies, Dzigar Kongtrül teaches the nonviolent practice of simmering. He says that rather than "boil in our aggression like a piece of meat cooking in a soup," we simmer in it. We allow ourselves to wait, to sit patiently with the urge to act or speak in our usual ways and feel the full force of that urge without turning away or giving in. Neither repressing nor rejecting, we stay in the middle between the two extremes, in the middle between yes and no, right and wrong, true and false. This is the journey of developing a kindhearted and courageous tolerance for our pain. Simmering is a way of gaining inner strength.

It helps us develop trust in ourselves—trust that we can experience the edginess, the groundlessness, the fundamental uncertainty of life and work with our mind, without acting in ways that are harmful to ourselves or others.

Before making the first commitment, we need to ask ourselves if we're ready to do something different. Are we sick to death of our same old repetitive patterns? Do we want to allow the space for new possibilities to emerge? The habit of escape is very strong, but are we ready to acknowledge when we're hooked? Are we willing to know our triggers and not respond habitually? Are we ready to open to uncertainty—or at least to give it a wholehearted try? If we can answer yes to any of these, then we're ready to take this vow.

With the commitment to not cause harm, we move away from reacting in ways that cause us to suffer, but we haven't yet arrived at a place that feels entirely relaxed and free. We first have to go through a growing-up process, a getting-used-to process. That process, that transition, is one of becoming comfortable with exactly what we're feeling as we feel it. The key practice to support us in this is mindfulness—being fully present right here, right now. Meditation is one form of mindfulness, but mindfulness is called by many names: *attentiveness, nowness,* and *presence* are just a few. Essentially, mindfulness means wakefulness—fully present wakefulness. Chögyam Trungpa called it paying attention to all the details of your life.

The specific details of our lives will, of course, differ, but for all of us, wakefulness concerns everything from how we make dinner to how we speak to one another to how we take care of our clothes, our floors, our forks and spoons. Just as with the other aspects of this commitment, we're either present when putting on our sweater or tying our shoes or brushing our teeth, or we're not. We're either awake or asleep, conscious or distracted. The contrast is pretty obvious. Chögyam Trungpa emphasized mindfulness and paying attention to the details of our lives as ways to develop appreciation for ourselves and our world, ways to free ourselves from suffering.

You build inner strength through embracing the totality of your experience, both the delightful parts and the difficult parts. Embracing the totality of your experience is one definition of having loving-kindness for yourself. Loving-kindness for yourself does not mean making sure you're feeling good all the time—trying to set up your life so that you're comfortable every moment. Rather, it means setting up your life so that you have time for meditation and self-reflection, for kindhearted, compassionate self-honesty. In this way you become more attuned to seeing when you're biting the hook, when you're getting caught in the undertow of emotions, when you're grasping and when you're letting go. This is the way you become a true friend to yourself just as you are, with both your laziness and your bravery. There is no step more important than this.

It's a tricky business—not rejecting any part of yourself at the same time that you're becoming acutely aware of how embarrassing or painful some of those parts are. What most of us have been doing is gearing our lives toward avoiding unpleasant feelings while clinging to whatever we think will make us feel good and feel secure. From a conventional point of view, this makes perfect sense. But from the vantage point of remaining with our direct experience, the vantage point of opening to the tentativeness of life, this strategy is self-defeating, the very thing that keeps us stuck.

There's an exercise that can help us reflect on this knee-jerk tendency to cling to what makes us feel good and push away what makes us feel bad:

Sit quietly for a few minutes and become mindful of your breath as it goes in and out. Then contemplate what you do when you're unhappy or dissatisfied and want to feel better. Even make a list if you want to. Then ask yourself: Does it work? Has it ever worked? Does it soothe the pain? Does it escalate the pain? If you're really honest, you'll come up with some pretty interesting observations.

One of the insights many people have when they do this exercise is yes, those efforts to make myself feel good *do* work—but not for very long. And the reason they stop working is that our strategies contain an inherent contradiction. We try to hold on to fleeting pleasures and avoid discomfort in a world where everything is always changing. Our strategies are not dependable. How we go about trying to feel secure and happy is at odds with the facts of life.

There's a Buddhist teaching called the eight worldly concerns that describes this predicament. It points out our main preoccupations in life—what drives us, what we hope for, what we fear. It points out how we continually try to avoid the uncertainty inherent in our condition, how we continually try to get solid ground under our feet. The eight worldly concerns are presented as four pairs of opposites: pleasure and pain, gain and loss, fame and disgrace, praise and blame.

Pleasure and pain drive us all the time. The attraction is simple: we want pleasure; we don't want pain. Our attachment to them is very strong, very visceral at either extreme. We can get that clenching-in-the-gut feeling of being hooked both when we crave something—when we're consumed with wanting or needing—and when we're averse to something and try to push it away.

We can spend a lifetime chasing after pleasure and trying to get away from pain, never staying present with the underlying feeling of discontent. But at some point it might hit us that there's more to liberation than trying to avoid discomfort, more to lasting happiness than pursuing temporary pleasures, temporary relief.

Our attachment to gain and loss also keeps us running in the rat race. So we shed the light of mindfulness on our shenpa to what we have or want and our equally strong shenpa to what we don't have or might lose. For instance, the money we have and the money we don't have preoccupy both the rich and the poor—and just about everyone in between—in countries all over the world.

Recently I met a woman who had unexpectedly inherited five hundred thousand dollars. She was understandably ecstatic. She invested it and gleefully watched it grow, until the stock market crashed and she lost it all as suddenly as she had gained it. After two months of deep depression (she said she was almost catatonic and couldn't eat or sleep), she had a revelation. It dawned on her that financially, she had been reasonably comfortable all along. She was fine before she hit the jackpot, and she was equally fine now that her newfound fortune was lost. It was her discovery of fundamental all-rightness, untouched by gain and loss, that she was overjoyed to report.

Gain and loss can also relate to the possessions we have or don't have and the drive to acquire things (shopping therapy, as some call it), as well as to the position in life we have or don't have. Competition—often cutthroat competition—is painfully visible in our society today. We see it in politics, in sports, in business, even in friendships. We also see its painful consequences.

At Gampo Abbey, we try a different approach. Every July 1—Canada's national day—we have a baseball game with the local Pleasant Bay Fire Department. We train for months ahead, and everybody plays with their whole heart—the firemen with their beers, us with our robes—but neither side really cares whether they win or lose. We all just have a great time without the suffering that's inevitable when we're entangled in loss and gain.

Fame and disgrace definitely snare us. Not many people are in a position to become famous, but this pairing can translate as wanting a good reputation—wanting people to think well of us—and not wanting a bad reputation. For most of us, this feeling runs very deep. For some of us, everything we do and say is to ensure that we'll be well thought of, that we'll be admired and won't be scorned.

Shantideva says that reputation is about as flimsy as a child's sand castle. We build it up, decorate it beautifully, and take great pride in it, but at the turn of the tide it all gets swept away. It's like the good reputation of politicians or spiritual teachers that is lost overnight because of sexual misconduct.

And even when fame *is* achieved, does it bring the happiness that people anticipate? Consider how common it is to have wealth and fame but be miserable, like Michael Jackson, Marilyn Monroe, and Elvis. What if, by contrast, we trained in staying in the middle—in that nongrasping open space between seeking what's comfortable and avoiding what's not?

Finally, let's consider our attachment to praise and blame. We want to be complimented and we don't want to be criticized. Some people blossom when they receive kudos for a job well done but go to pieces when they receive criticism, even if it's constructive. Young children, teenagers, and yes, even the most mature of adults can have their spirits lifted up by compliments and cast down by criticism. We are so easily blown about by the winds of praise and blame.

> This has been going on through the ages. They criticize the silent ones. They criticize the talkative ones. They criticize the moderate ones. There is no one in the world that escapes criticism. There never was and never will be, nor is there now, the wholly criticized or the wholly approved.

Shakyamuni Buddha said that more than twenty-five hundred years ago, but it seems that some things never change.

In one way or another, we're all hooked by our attachment to the eight worldly concerns. Dzigar Kongtrül once said it's as if we have a split personality: we can think we're committed to a spiritual path, but sadly, we're equally committed to the eight worldly concerns, to accepting what's comfortable and rejecting what's not. This gets us nowhere fast. Without that split personality, however, our commitment to waking up becomes wholehearted. We stop being blinded by the eight worldly concerns and stay present with the underlying discomfort.

When we decide to work with the commitment to not cause harm, we have to investigate how seduced we are by the eight worldly concerns. Are we willing to go to any lengths to free ourselves from the tyranny of pleasure and pain, of what people think, of whether we win or lose, of whether we have a good or bad reputation? It doesn't matter how far we get with freeing ourselves before we die. What matters is that we make the journey.

After he was diagnosed with cancer, the visionary genius Steve Jobs had this to say about freedom from the eight worldly concerns:

> Remembering that I'll be dead soon is the most important tool I've ever encountered to help me make the big choices in life. Because almost everything— all external expectations, all pride, all fear of embarrassment or failure—these things just fall away in the face of death, leaving only what is truly important. Remembering that you are going to die is the best way I know to avoid the trap of thinking you have something to lose. You are already naked. There is no reason not to follow your heart.

The first commitment is a vow to know your triggers, a vow that whatever it takes, you'll compassionately acknowledge when you're hooked by the eight worldly concerns—or, indeed, hooked by anything. When you look at what gets to you, it will undoubtedly have something to do with what you want or do not want. Whenever you realize you're caught, right then, right on the spot, with kindness for yourself, you can acknowledge that you're hooked. And then you can ask yourself: Which of the eight worldly concerns has me in its grip? Fear of loss? Hope of gain? The pain of being blamed? The desire to be praised? And who's in control here—me or the eight worldly concerns?

We can't even acknowledge what's happening, however, if we're caught up in our thoughts—in worrying and planning and fantasizing. That's why we continue to train in meditation, noticing when we're lost in thought and then coming back to this very moment.

I had an experience a few years ago of being liberated from the tyranny of the eight worldly concerns. At that time I was living at a retreat center along with nine other people, and every afternoon we would get together for a work period. This was a painful time for me because there was almost nothing I could do. I couldn't haul water because of my bad back. I couldn't paint decks because of environmental sensitivities. I was essentially useless in that situation, and it was extremely irritating to the work leader. I felt old, feeble, incompetent, and disliked. I felt really miserable.

This led me to some deep contemplation: If I wasn't the well-respected, accomplished spiritual teacher I'd grown accustomed to being, then who was I? Without the outer confirmation, without the labels, who was I? I talked to Dzigar Kongtrül about my concern, and he asked me, "Isn't it a big relief?" I had to be honest and say, "Not yet."

Then a few of us were invited to attend some spiritual teachings in town. As soon as we arrived, I started to be treated as a special person. I had a special high seat, a special glass of water, a special place in the front row.

Seeing the dramatic difference in how I was perceived snapped some deep attachment I had to fame and disgrace, to loss and gain, to hope and fear about my identity. Up the mountain at the retreat center I was nobody. Down the mountain at the teaching I was a special guest, worthy of respect. But these were just shifting, ambiguous labels.

Fundamentally, I couldn't ever be pinpointed, couldn't ever be labeled definitively. At that moment, I genuinely felt the relief that Dzigar Kongtrül had asked me about.

The eight worldly concerns are, at bottom, just an outdated mechanism for survival. In that sense, we're still functioning at a very primitive level, completely at the mercy of hope and fear. The mechanism of avoiding pain and seeking pleasure kept us from being eaten, kept us from freezing to death in winter, kept us figuring out how to get food and how to clothe ourselves. This worked well for our ancestors, but it isn't working very well for us now. In fact, we continually overreact when it's hardly a life-or-death matter. We behave as if our very existence were threatened, when all that's at stake is maybe a late charge. We're like Ping-Pong balls being bounced back and forth by our aversions and desires, and we're way overdue for trying a fresh alternative.

In the year 2000 the elders of the Hopi Nation made a prediction about the future and offered advice on how to live in the upcoming millennium. The Hopi elders are considered the earth protectors, the ones who are responsible for the survival (or not) of our planet. They said that we were now in a fast-flowing river and that many of us would be afraid and try to cling to the shore. But those who cling to the shore, they said, "will suffer greatly." The advice of the elders was to let go of the shore and push off into the middle of the river, see who was there with us—"and celebrate."

Refraining but not repressing, contemplating our personal experience of being caught, acknowledging our triggers, the nonviolent practice of simmering—all of these are ways of letting go of the shore and pushing off into the middle of the river. All of these are ways of allowing ourselves to live free of story lines, free of crippling attachments to what we want and don't want, free of fixed mind and self-centeredness. If we don't act on our craving for pleasure or our fear of pain, we're left in the wide-open, unpredictable middle. The instruction is to rest in that vulnerable place, to rest in that in-between state, to not hunker down and stay fixed in our belief systems but to take a fresh look with a wider perspective.

The truth is that we're always in some kind of in-between state, always in process. We never fully arrive. When we're present with the dynamic quality of our lives, we're also present with impermanence, uncertainty, and change. If we can stay present, then we might finally get that there's no security or certainty in the objects of our pleasure or the objects of our pain, no security or certainty in winning or losing, in compliments or criticism, in good reputation or bad—no security or certainty ever in anything that's fleeting, that's subject to change.

The commitment to not cause harm is very clear-cut. The only way to break it is to speak or act out of a confused mind. The simplicity and clarity of this commitment helps us build an unshakable foundation of inner strength. This manifests as the courage to take a chance, the courage not to act in the same old ways. It builds confidence in our ability to cultivate renunciation at the deepest level and in our ability to see shenpa when it arises and realize when we're once again caught in the eight worldly concerns. It builds confidence in our ability to live without a game plan, to live unfettered by hope and fear. When people make this commitment, they begin to change. You might run into them after a year or two and find that something in them has softened. They seem more at home with themselves and the world, more flexible and easier to get along with.

At some point, if you're fortunate, you'll hit a wall of truth and wonder what you've been doing with your life. At that point you'll feel highly motivated to find out what frees you and helps you to be kinder and more loving, less klesha driven and confused. At that point you'll actually want to be present—present as you go through a door, present as you take a step, present as you wash your hands or wash a dish, present to being triggered, present to simmering, present to the ebb and flow of your emotions and thoughts. Day in and day out, you'll find that you notice sooner when you're hooked, and it will be easier to refrain. If you continue to do this, a kind of shedding happens—a shedding of old habits, a shedding of being run around by pleasure and pain, a shedding of being held hostage by the eight worldly concerns.

Awakening is not a process of building ourselves up but a process of letting go. It's a process of relaxing in the middle—the paradoxical, ambiguous middle, full of potential, full of new ways of thinking and seeing—with absolutely no money-back guarantee of what will happen next.

The Second Commitment
Committing to Take Care of One Another

Taking the . . . vow to help others implies that instead of
holding our own individual territory and defending it
tooth and nail, we become open to the world that we are
living in. It means we are willing to take on greater
responsibility, immense responsibility. In fact, it
means taking a big chance.

—Chögyam Trungpa Rinpoche

6

Beyond Our Comfort Zone

COMPASSION IS THREATENING to the ego. We might think of it as something warm and soothing, but actually it's very raw. When we set out to support other beings, when we go so far as to stand in their shoes, when we aspire to never close down to anyone, we quickly find ourselves in the uncomfortable territory of "life not on my terms." The second commitment, traditionally known as the Bodhisattva Vow, or warrior vow, challenges us to dive into these noncozy waters and swim out beyond our comfort zone.

Our willingness to make the first commitment is our initial step toward relaxing completely with uncertainty and change. The commitment is to refrain from speech and action that would be harmful to ourselves and others and then to make friends with the underlying feelings that motivate us to do harm in the first place. The second commitment builds on this foundation: we vow to move consciously into the pain of the world in order to help alleviate it. It is, in essence, a vow to take care of one another, even if it sometimes means not liking how that feels.

The second commitment is connected deeply and unshakably with *bodhicitta*, traditionally defined as a longing to awaken so that we can help others do the same, a longing to go beyond the limits of conventional happiness, beyond enslavement to success and failure, praise and blame.

Bodhicitta is also a trust in our innate ability to go beyond bias, beyond prejudice and fixed opinions, and open our hearts to everyone: those we like, those we don't like, those we don't even notice, those we may never meet. Bodhicitta counteracts our tendency to stay stuck in very narrow thinking. It counteracts our resistance to change.

This degree of openness arises from the trust that we all have basic goodness and that we can interact with one another in ways that bring that out. Instead of reacting aggressively when we're provoked, endlessly perpetuating the cycle of pain, we trust that we can engage with others from a place of curiosity and caring and in that way contact their innate decency and wisdom.

A friend who works in a department store decided some years ago that she would test her belief that everyone is basically good. She wanted to see if she could find anyone she felt was not a candidate. Every day she encountered friendly people, for sure, but also plenty of rude people, arrogant people, manipulative people, and downright mean-spirited people. In each case, she experimented with ways to go beneath their facades, to go past their defenses and contact their good sense, their humor, and their kindness. When we last talked, she hadn't yet met anyone she felt lacked basic goodness, and she's been working at that store for fifteen years.

With the first commitment we begin to build confidence in our ability to embrace the raw, edgy, unpredictable energy of life. With the second commitment we step further into groundlessness as a source of awakening rather than a source of dread, as a path to fearlessness rather than a threat to our survival. If we haven't already been training in relaxing with fundamental uneasiness, then making the second commitment can be terrifying, because we're moving deeper into this open-ended, undefined territory called benefiting others.

Committing to benefit others is traditionally called the path of the bodhisattva, the path of the hero and heroine, the path of the spiritual warrior whose weapons are gentleness, clarity of mind, and an open heart. The Tibetan word for warrior, *pawo* for a male warrior or *pawmo* for a female warrior, means "the one who cultivates bravery." As warriors in training, we cultivate the courage and flexibility to live with uncertainty—with the shaky, tender feeling of anxiety, of nothing to hold on to—and to dedicate our lives to making ourselves available to every person, in every situation.

The commitment to take care of one another is often described as a vow to invite all sentient beings to be our guest. The prospect can be daunting. It means that everyone will be coming to our house. It means opening our door to everyone, not just to the people we like or the ones who smell good or the ones we consider "proper" but also to the violent ones and the confused ones—to people of all shapes, sizes, and colors, to people speaking all different languages, to people with all different points of view. Making the second commitment means holding a diversity party in our living room, all day every day, until the end of time.

Initially, most of us are in no way ready to commit to all of that—we are in no way ready to leap into that much groundlessness without reservation. But if we have a longing to alleviate suffering, what can we do? For one thing, we can invite everybody and open the door to them all, but open the door only briefly at first. We open it only for as long as we're currently able to and give ourselves permission to close it when we become too uncomfortable. However, our aspiration is always to open the door again and to keep it open for a few seconds longer than the time before.

When we practice this way, the results may be surprising. In opening the door gradually, not trying to throw it open all at once, we get used to the shaky feeling we experience when people we can't quite handle start coming to the party. Rather than thinking, *I have to open the door completely or I'm not doing it right,* we start with the strong intention to keep opening that door, and bit by bit, we tap into a reservoir of inner strength and courage that we never knew we had.

Opening the door reflects our intention to remove our armor, to take off our mask, to face our fears. It is only to the degree that we become willing to face our own feelings that we can really help others. So we make a commitment that for the rest of our lives, we'll train in freeing ourselves from the tyranny of our own reactivity, our own survival mechanisms, our own propensities to be hooked.

It's not that we won't ever experience those feelings again. Fundamental uneasiness will continue to arise over and over, but when it does, we won't overreact to it, we won't let it rule our life. I once asked Dzigar Kongtrül about this, and he said, "Yes, I still have those feelings, but they don't catch me." He is, it seems, no longer afraid of fear.

Those raw feelings can even inspire us to action. When an interviewer asked the Dalai Lama if he had any regrets, he replied that yes, he did: he felt responsible for the death of an elderly monk who had come to him for guidance. When the interviewer asked how he had dealt with that feeling of regret, how he had gotten rid of it, His Holiness replied, "I didn't get rid of it. It's still there." But it no longer drags him down. It has motivated him to keep working to benefit people in every way he can.

The commitment to take care of one another is a vow to awaken so we can help other beings awaken. A vow to awaken so we can alleviate the suffering in the world. A vow to continue on this journey for as long as it takes, even if that's forever. Shantideva captures the essence of this commitment in a verse that's said to be a favorite of the Dalai Lama's:

And now as long as space endures,
As long as there are beings to be found,
May I continue likewise to remain
To drive away the sorrows of the world.

Given the vast scope of this second commitment, keeping it is like mission impossible. One way we break it is by closing our heart or mind to someone for even a few seconds. I've never known anyone who could avoid this altogether, but still we pledge to move toward keeping the door open to everyone. Another way we break the vow is through self-denigration—believing our own faults are intrinsic and impossible to remove and sending ourselves messages like "I'm a hopeless case; I'll never get it." We also break the vow when we denigrate others, criticizing their culture or customs or traditions or beliefs. Bias or bigotry of any sort breaks the vow.

When we break the first commitment, when we cause harm at the level of speech or action, it's very clear. If, for example, we kill or lie or steal, there's no question that we've broken the vow. But when it comes to the commitment to take care of one another, breaking the vow is not so straightforward. There is a traditional Buddhist tale that illustrates this point. A sea captain known as Captain Courage was piloting a ship carrying five hundred men when a pirate boarded the boat and threatened to kill them all. The captain realized that if the pirate carried out his plan, he would not only kill all the passengers but also sow the seeds of his own intense suffering. So, out of compassion for the pirate as well as to save the five hundred men, the captain killed the pirate. In killing one to save many, Captain Courage was willing to take the consequences of his actions, whatever they might be, in order to prevent the suffering of others. This is why the second commitment requires bravery—the bravery to do whatever we think will bring the greatest benefit, the bravery to face the fact that we never know for sure what will really benefit and what, in fact, will only make matters worse.

Few of us will ever be confronted with a predicament like Captain Courage's, of course, but we can easily find ourselves in situations in which we try to rationalize our questionable behavior with some perfectly plausible justification. It's amazing the levels of self-deception we can reach. But that's where the commitments are such a support. They help us to acknowledge our state of mind and pull ourselves out of a downward slide.

We don't graduate from one commitment to the next. The commitment to not cause harm stays in place as the foundation for the commitment to take care of one another. The training in not acting or speaking in a way that escalates suffering, the training in acknowledging our triggers and staying present with discomfort, is essential if we wish to go further. The commitment to not cause harm helps us cut through self-deception and develop a friendship with ourselves, a friendship that deepens as we begin to look closely at ourselves and lay aside the habits that cause us continued suffering. The warrior commitment rests on that base of self-honesty. When we meet our edge, when life triggers our habitual responses, we train in catching them, knowing that if we speak or act out of shenpa, we won't be able to respond appropriately and support others.

Fortunately, when we break the commitment to take care of one another, it's easy to mend. We start by acknowledging that we broke it, that we hardened our heart and closed our mind, that we shut someone out. And then we can retake our vow. On the spot—or as a daily practice— we can reaffirm our intention to keep the door open to all sentient beings for the rest of our life. That's the training of the spiritual warrior, the training of cultivating courage and empathy, the training of cultivating love. It would be impossible to count the number of beings in the world who are hurting, but still we aspire to not give up on any of them and to do whatever we can to alleviate their pain.

Needless to say, we probably won't do this perfectly. I once had the experience of sitting quietly on my bed, reading Shantideva and crying because I was so moved to be loving and compassionate. Then someone burst into the room, and I blew up at her for interrupting me.

Experiences like that are definitely humbling. They can either cause us to spin off into self-criticism or inspire us to renew our intention to be there for others, no matter what they trigger. Right then, when we miss the mark, we can do the three-step practice. We can use it to catch the spark of irritation, impatience, or disappointment before it bursts into the flames of anger. This practice allows us to look at what's happening around us while simultaneously being aware of what's happening inside us. To review the steps:

First, come into the present. Flash on what's happening with you right now. Be fully aware of your body, its energetic quality. Be aware of your thoughts and emotions.

Next, feel your heart, literally placing your hand on your chest if you find that helpful. This is a way of accepting yourself just as you are in that moment, a way of saying, "This is my experience right now, and it's okay."

Then go into the next moment without any agenda.

This practice can open us to others at times when we tend to close down. It gives us a way to be awake rather than asleep, a way to look outward rather than withdraw. For example, we often go into a meeting so preoccupied with what we're going to say that we tune out other people, not hearing what they're saying or picking up clues about how they're feeling. But if, before entering, we can ground ourselves by doing the three-step practice, bringing mind and body together right where we are, then we can enter the meeting with an open mind, an inquisitive "let's see how this unfolds" attitude, rather than being fixated on achieving a specific outcome. We prepare, we know our topic, and then we leap. This was how I was taught to teach. I read, I take notes, I decide what I want to say. And then I go into the room and speak without any props.

Many years ago, one of the monks at Gampo Abbey introduced me to the practice of saying to myself when I wake up, "I wonder what will happen today." That's the spirit of taking a leap.

As we continue to do this practice, whether as a formal meditation or on the spot throughout the day, we become more and more skilled at noticing when we're activated. So we come into the present—"synchronizing body and mind," as Chögyam Trungpa called it—then drop the story line and open to the person or situation at hand. This is the foundation for caring for one another, for extending ourselves to others with kindness and compassion. This is the practice of claiming our warriorship rather than being swept away by our thoughts and emotions.

Granted, there's a discrepancy between the inclusiveness of the second commitment and the reality that there are, for sure, people we have trouble liking. Boss, coworker, spouse, roommate, mother, father, child—who are the people you really dislike and wish would simply go away? Who's on your list? Be grateful to them: they're your own special gurus, showing up right on time to keep you honest. It's the troublemakers in your life who cause you to see that you've shut down, that you've armored yourself, that you've hidden your head in the sand. If you didn't get angry at them, if you didn't get fed up with them, you would never be able to cultivate patience. If you didn't envy them, if you weren't jealous of them, you would never think to stretch beyond your mean-spiritedness and try to rejoice in their good fortune. If you never met your match, you might think you were better than everybody else and arrogantly criticize their neurotic behavior rather than do something about your own.

When we make this commitment, we begin an ongoing

training in loving-kindness and compassion. One way to do this is to continually ask ourselves: How can I be of service? We can make this an everyday practice. Time after time, however, we'll find that we're not really sure what will help and not hurt. But the warrior learns a lot by failing. We probably learn more from our mistakes than from our successes. We have to recognize when something doesn't work and—this is important—not take it personally. Instead, we can follow Chögyam Trungpa's suggestion: *Live your life as an experiment.* Adopt an attitude of "I'm not sure what will help in this situation, but I'm going to experiment and try this." Sometimes the result will be, "Wow, did *that* ever not work!" But if it is, we've learned something. And now we can try something else.

In our efforts to keep this commitment, it helps to give ourselves a break and remember the enormity of it—the time frame, which is so long that it's unimaginable, and the number of people we vow to help, which is infinite: not just people we feel sorry for but all beings everywhere, without exception. If we see them on the street, if we read about them in the news, if we hear about them from our friends—if they come into our consciousness in any way—they are candidates for our loving-kindness and compassion. It's an assignment without boundaries, without borders, and we're forever engaged in on-the-job training.

The aspiration of the warrior is to not close down ever—even when a personal relationship falters. That's not to say there won't be pain involved. The ending of a previously close relationship throws us right into the midst of fundamental uncertainty—and that definitely hurts. We've met our edge. We find ourselves caught up in behaviors we assumed we had outgrown years ago. Sometimes just the thought of the person makes us close down. But often it is a seemingly irresolvable relationship that teaches us the most, once we're willing to be vulnerable and honest, once we're willing to connect with what Chögyam Trungpa called "the genuine heart of sadness." As warriors in training we do our best to hold the person in our heart without any hypocrisy. One thing we can do with a difficult relationship is to place a picture of the person somewhere we will see it often and think, *I wish for your deepest well-being.* Or we can write down the person's name, along with the aspiration that they may be safe, may be happy, may live in peace.

Regardless of what specific action we take, our aspiration is to benefit the other person and wish them well. This aspiration is based on a growing trust in basic goodness, our own and theirs. It's based on our willingness to shed our own protective layers and try to see the other person free of our labels and fixed ideas. We try to drop the story line about how that person harmed us, about how they're at fault. We still may be left with the rawness of our feelings, with our aversion to the person and to the situation. But regardless of what happened, regardless of who did what to whom, we do whatever we can to dissolve our negativity. That doesn't necessarily mean getting back together—often it means staying away—but we can send the person forgiveness and caring. Believe me, that feels a whole lot better than poisoning ourselves with bitterness.

The task is inconceivable: saving everyone everywhere from endless depths of suffering. Not just from hunger or no clothes or no shelter, or from being abused or neglected or tortured or killed. We also dedicate our lives to saving both ourselves and others from the very causes of suffering: from our tendencies to cause harm and escalate aggression, from our inability to know our triggers or see our prejudices, from our preexisting propensities to be provoked and then blame it all on other people.

With the warrior commitment we gradually become a vehicle for connecting others with their unfettered mind, with their intrinsic goodness, so that they, too, can begin to embrace the groundlessness of being human as a source of inspiration and joy. Our wish for all beings, including ourselves, is to live fearlessly with uncertainty and change. The compassion and kindness required for this are limitless, but we start with whatever we have right now and build on that.

The warrior commitment involves understanding that there is nothing static about human beings. Usually we try hard to maintain our fixed ideas about people: my self-centered, unreasonable sister; my cheerful, optimistic coworker; my mean, uptight father. And what about me? I'm too fat, a loser, can never get it right; I'm a lot smarter than everyone else, or in better shape; I'm capable and successful; I'm not cut out to be a meditator; I'm a bad mother and a worse spouse. But in fact, we can't make a single label stick. We can't ever conclude definitively what someone is like, because the data is always changing. The information is never all in.

This commitment challenges us to question our conventional mind-set, question reality as we usually assume it to be. Each of us lives in a reality we take to be the real one. This is how it is, we insist. End of story. But isn't even the consensus reality we share as human beings just a projection of our human sense perceptions? Animals don't have the same perceptions as we do; therefore, they don't share the same reality. So what is the "real" reality? Is it ours? Is it a dog's? A bird's? A fly's? The answer is, there isn't one "real" reality. Reality is wherever we find ourselves in the moment, and it's not as solid, not as certain, as we think.

One of the astronauts who went to the moon later described his experience looking back at Earth from that perspective. Earth looked so small, he said. Just a single sphere hanging in space. It made him very sad to realize that we have divided the world arbitrarily into countries that we're fiercely attached to, with borders we keep waging wars to protect. What we do just doesn't make sense, he realized. We have just this one Earth with one people to take care of it, and the way we're going about it is crazy.

Chief Seattle had the same insight more than a hundred years ago:

> We are all children of the Great Spirit. We all belong to Mother Earth. Our planet is in great trouble, and if we keep carrying old grudges and do not work together, we will all die.

The way we label things is the way they will appear to us. When we label a piece of the earth *China* or *Brazil* or the *United States,* it becomes an entity that carries strong emotional baggage. When we label something *good,* we see it as good. When we label something *bad,* we see it as bad. We get so hung up on like and dislike, on who's right and who's wrong, as if these labels were ultimately real. Yet the human experience is an experience of nothing to hang on to, nothing that's set once and for all. Reality is always falling apart. In this fleeting situation, the only thing that makes sense is for us to reach out to one another.

As we move in the direction of seeing more space around

our fixed ideas, around our limited sense of self, around our notions of right and wrong, around the labels we're so invested in, the crack in our conventional way of experiencing life will get wider and wider. At that point it may start to dawn on us that if we want to change the movie of our life, we will have to change our mind.

There's a story that Ed Brown, the Zen chef, tells about his early days with his teacher, Suzuki Roshi. Ed was the head cook at Tassajara Zen Mountain Center in California in the 1960s and was well known for his volatile temper. Once, in a fury, he went to his teacher and complained about the state of the kitchen: people didn't clean up properly; people talked too much; people were distracted and unmindful. It was chaos on a daily basis. Suzuki Roshi's reply was simple: "Ed, if you want a calm kitchen, calm your mind."

If your mind is expansive and unfettered, you will find yourself in a more accommodating world, a place that's endlessly interesting and alive. That quality isn't inherent in the place but in your state of mind. The warrior longs to communicate that all of us have access to our basic goodness and that genuine freedom comes from going beyond labels and projections, beyond bias and prejudice, and taking care of each other.

7

Breathing In Pain,
Breathing Out Relief

On September 11, 2001, the bottom fell out for millions of people. When the two planes flew into the Twin Towers of the World Trade Center, life as many of us knew it changed forever. There was a societal experience of groundlessness. The truth of uncertainty and change was very immediate for those living in New York City, for those living all over the United States, and for many people around the world.

In the days that followed, in this all-pervasive atmosphere of not knowing what was happening or what to do, large groups gathered in cities and towns throughout America to do a practice called *tonglen*. The instruction was to breathe in as deeply as possible the pain and fear of all of those who had been in the burning towers, all of those who had jumped to their death, all of those in the airplanes, and all the millions traumatized by this event. And also to breathe in the anger of the hijackers and those who had planned the attack. And then to breathe out, sending relief to them all.

Some sent love and care to all who were suffering. Some sent coolness and an escape from the scorching heat of the flames to those who had been trapped in the towers and planes. Some sent fearlessness. Some sent the aspiration that no one would hold feelings of hatred or rage. Breathing in, all of them did the only thing they could to support those who hadn't survived. Breathing out, they found a way to put into practice a deep longing to be of help, whatever that might mean. Of course, thousands of people in New York City and elsewhere immediately volunteered their support. In fact, there was such a flood of volunteers that many had to be turned away. But no one was turned away from the tonglen gatherings, and people who could not help in any other way joined with many others whose intention was to ease the suffering of those who had died in unimaginable pain and those they had left behind.

Tonglen is a core practice for warriors in training, the most effective tool for developing courage and arousing our sense of oneness with others. It's a practice for staying in the middle of the river. It gives us the strength to let go of the shore.

There are various ways that tonglen is taught, but the essence of it is breathing in that which is unpleasant and unwanted and breathing out—sending out—that which is pleasing, relieving, enjoyable. In other words, we breathe in the things we usually try to avoid, such as our sadness and anger, and we send out the things we usually cling to, such as our happiness and good health. We breathe in pain and send out pleasure. We breathe in disgrace and send out good reputation. We breathe in loss and send out gain. This is an exceedingly counterhabitual practice. It helps us overcome our fear of suffering and tap into the compassion that's inherent in us all.

The word *tonglen* is Tibetan for "sending and receiving." It refers to our willingness to take on the pain of others we know are hurting and extend to them whatever we feel will ease their pain, whatever will enable them to stay present with the sorrows and losses and disappointments of life.

Practicing tonglen awakens our natural empathy, our innate ability to put ourselves in others' shoes. Caring about people when they're scared or sad or angry or arrogant can be a challenge; it confronts us with our own pain and fear, with the places where we're stuck. But if we can stay with those unwanted feelings, we can use them as stepping-stones to understanding the pain and fear of others. Tonglen allows us to acknowledge where we are in the moment and, at the same time, cultivate a sense of kinship with others. When painful feelings arise, we breathe them in, opening to our own suffering and the suffering of everyone else who is feeling the same way. Then we send relief to us all.

This is the style of tonglen that has been the most liberating for me. It uses the very immediate and unsettling rawness of our own discomfort as a link to others. It allows us to understand in an experiential, nonconceptual way that our suffering is not unique but is shared by millions and trillions of other beings, animal as well as human. We find out that we have cancer, and we breathe in the fear, the disbelief, the pain of all cancer patients and send relief to all. We lose someone dear to us, and it connects us to everyone who is overcome with grief. We lie awake with insomnia, and it links us to countless others who are lying awake. On the spot, we breathe in our sleeplessness and the sleeplessness of others, breathe in our anxiety, our agitation, and the same discomfort felt by others. On the spot, we send out restfulness, peace of mind, contentment—even a visualization of all of us sleeping soundly.

Tonglen is a practice for thinking bigger, for touching into our sameness with all beings. Instead of withdrawing into ourselves, we can use the grittiness, the harshness of the human condition as a way to rouse our natural ability to love, to care, to understand our interconnectedness. With tonglen, our misfortunes become a means to awaken our heart, enabling us to work wholeheartedly for the sake of others and at the same time be a true friend to ourselves.

Tonglen isn't just a practice to do on the meditation cushion. It's particularly useful right in the midst of our life, wherever we are as we go about the day. Maybe a letter or an e-mail arrives from a friend who's having a hard time, who's depressed, who's grieving an upsetting loss. Right then, you can start breathing in your friend's pain, connecting with his sadness or despair and wishing for his suffering to lift. Then, as you exhale, you can send him relief—joy, caring, peace of mind, or whatever seems most appropriate.

Perhaps you're out on the street and see someone abusing a dog, beating it or yelling at it or yanking on its leash. You can breathe in the pain you assume the dog is feeling, then send out relief. It might be a wish for the dog to experience kindness and safety, even a nice, juicy bone. You can also breathe in what the abuser is likely to be feeling—the rage and confusion that are causing her to strike out so cruelly. Breathe in her anger and, on the out breath, send her anything you think would allow her heart to soften. It could be feeling loved, feeling okay about herself, feeling more space in her mind and more tenderness in her heart.

Tonglen is especially useful when we get into a conflict with someone and feel our own pain and confusion rising. Let's say you walk into a room and someone says something you don't like or gives you a nasty look. Ordinarily you might shut down or go blank or obsess about getting even, or whatever you do to exit when you don't want to deal with painful feelings. With tonglen, however, you can work with the emotions right then. Maybe you're feeling fear. You can open yourself completely to it—the smell of it, the texture of it, the tension in your body—and breathe it all in. As you continue to breathe in fear, you can open to include everyone everywhere who's afraid. You can even stretch your limit and include the person who triggered your fear, with the wish that he or she be free of suffering. Then, as you breathe out, you can send out an aspiration for all beings who are feeling fear, yourself included, to be free of it.

Right on the spot, you own your feelings completely. Instead of pushing the emotions away, you're completely in touch with them. This isn't the same as being self-absorbed, caught up only in your own distress. Far from it. Tonglen puts us in touch with all the others who are just like us, who feel the way we do. We all experience pain and pleasure. We all gravitate to what's comfortable and have an aversion to what's not.

Often people ask me, "But how do I know that other people are feeling the same thing I am?" I think it's safe to say that there's almost nothing we feel that millions of other people aren't also feeling—or haven't felt at some time. Our story lines are different, but when it comes to pain and pleasure and our reaction to them, people everywhere are the same.

Tonglen goes against the grain of how we usually deal with the world: wanting life on our own terms, wanting things to work out for our own benefit, no matter what happens to others. The practice begins to break down the walls we've built around ourselves, begins to liberate us from the prison of self. As this protective shield starts to come apart, we naturally feel a wish to reach out. People need help, and we can provide it—both literally and at the level of aspiration for their well-being.

Tonglen reverses the usual logic of avoiding suffering and seeking pleasure. To the degree that we can open to our own pain, we can open to the pain of others. To the degree that we can stay present with our own pain, we can hang in with someone who's provoking us. We come to see pain as something that can transform us, not as something to escape at any cost. As we continue to practice tonglen, our compassion is bound to grow. We'll find ourselves increasingly more able to be there for others, even in what used to seem like impossible situations.

Not that there won't be times when we simply can't do the practice. It may be that when we're confronted with suffering, our own or someone else's, we can't face it, so we go numb. Or we may have no problem getting in touch with pain, but we can't send out relief. The situation may seem so overwhelming that we can't think of any form of relief that would make a dent in what we're witnessing or feeling. But whatever the reason we can't do tonglen, it isn't grounds for self-criticism or despair. Life is full of opportunities for us to try again.

Resistance of any sort points to how important it is to bring a sense of spaciousness to this practice. One way to do this is to imagine that you're breathing into a space as vast as the sky. If you sense your body as boundless, transparent, and big enough to accommodate any amount of suffering, you can breathe in knowing that there is nowhere for the pain to get stuck. Then, as you breathe out, you can send out that same feeling of openness and freedom, the feeling that there's lots of room, unlimited room, enough room to accommodate anything—misery, delight, the whole gamut of human emotions.

As a formal meditation practice, tonglen has four stages:

The first stage is a pause, a moment of stillness and space, a brief gap. If you need an image for this, you can reflect on any experience of wide-open space, such as gazing out at the ocean or looking up into a cloudless sky.

The second stage is a visualization, working with texture. As you inhale, breathe in hot, heavy, thick energy—a feeling of claustrophobia. Breathe it in completely, through all the pores of your body. Then, as you exhale, breathe out a sense of freshness, of cool, light, bright energy. Radiate it outward 360 degrees. Continue for a few minutes, or until the imagery is in sync with the in and out breaths.

The third stage involves breathing in a specific painful situation, opening to it as fully as possible, then breathing out spaciousness and relief. Traditionally we begin tonglen for a person or animal we wish to help, but we can also begin with our personal experience in the moment—a feeling of hopelessness or anger, for example—and use that as a stepping-stone for connecting us with the painful feelings of others.

In the fourth stage, we extend tonglen further. If we're doing it for a friend with AIDS, we extend it to all of those with AIDS. If we're doing it for our alcoholic sister, we extend it to all alcoholics, to all of those suffering from addiction. If we're already doing tonglen for all of those experiencing the same pain that we are, we can extend it to all of those, all over the world, who are suffering in any way, mentally or physically. And we can extend it still further to include all of us caught up in self-absorption, all of us tormented by our fixated minds and our inability to let go of hope and fear.

As a general guideline, we start tonglen practice with a situation that is immediate and real, not something vague or impersonal. Then we extend it to include more and more beings who are suffering in a similar way, as well as all of us suffering from ego clinging, all of us suffering from resistance to uncertainty and impermanence.

If we ourselves have had even a glimmer of what egolessness feels like, of what awakening feels like, of what freedom feels like, then we want that for others too. When we see that they're hooked, instead of being critical and judgmental, we can empathize with what they're going through—we've been there and know exactly how they feel. Our wish for other people is the same as our wish for ourselves: to appreciate ourselves, to recognize when we're caught and disentangle ourselves from those feelings, to stop reinforcing the dysfunctional patterns that prolong our suffering, to reach out to others, to experience the goodness of being human.

Whether we do tonglen as a formal practice or on the spot, does it take time to get used to? Yes, it does. Does it take getting accustomed to the rawness of pain? Does it take patience and gentleness? Yes, it does. There's no need to get discouraged when the practice seems too hard. Allow yourself to ease into it slowly at your own pace, working first with situations that are easy for you right now. I always remember what Chögyam Trungpa used to say when I was losing my confidence and wanted to give up. He'd sit up tall and smile broadly and proclaim, "You can do it!" Somehow his confidence was contagious, and when I heard those words, I knew I could.

I once read a poem about practicing tonglen in a time of war. The imagery was of breathing in bombs falling, violence, despair, losing your legs and coming home with your face burned and disfigured, and then sending out the beauty of the earth and sky, the goodness of people, safety and peace. In the same spirit, we can breathe in hatred and jealousy, envy and addiction—all the sorrow of the human drama—using our personal experience of that pain and extending tonglen to all others caught in the same way. Then we can breathe out flexibility, lightheartedness, nonaggression, strength—whatever we feel will bring comfort and upliftedness and relief. The pain of the world pierces us to the heart, but we never forget the goodness of being alive.

Chögyam Trungpa once said, "The problem with most people is that they are always trying to give out the bad and take in the good. That has been the problem of society in general and the world altogether." The time has come for us to try the opposite approach: to take in the bad and give out the good. Compassion is not a matter of pity or the strong helping the weak; it's a relationship between equals, one of mutual support. Practicing tonglen, we come to realize that other people's welfare is just as important as our own. In helping them, we help ourselves. In helping ourselves, we help the world.

8

The Catalyst for Compassion

SOMEONE SENT ME a poem that seems to capture the essence of the warrior commitment—empathy for other beings. Called "Birdfoot's Grampa," the poem is about a boy and his grandfather who are driving on a country road in a rainstorm. The grandfather keeps stopping the car and getting out to scoop up handfuls of toads that are all over the road and deposit them safely at the roadside. After the twenty-fourth time he's done this, the boy loses patience and tells his grandfather, "You can't save them all / accept it, get back in / we've got places to go." And the grandfather, knee deep in wet grass, his hands full of toads, just smiles at his grandson and says, "They have places to go too."

What a clear illustration of how this commitment works. The grandfather didn't mind stopping for the twenty-fourth time, didn't mind getting wet to save the toads. He also didn't mind the impatience of his grandson, because he was very clear in his mind that the frogs had as much desire to live as he did.

The aspiration of the second commitment—to care for all beings everywhere—is huge. But whether we're making this commitment for the very first time or we're renewing it for the umpteenth time, we start exactly where we are now. We're either closer to the grandson or closer to the grandfather, but wherever we are, that's where we start.

It's said that when we make this commitment, it sows a seed deep in our unconscious, deep in our mind and heart, that never goes away. This seed is a catalyst that jump-starts our inherent capacity for love and compassion, for empathy, for seeing the sameness of us all. So we make the commitment, we sow the seed, and then do our best to never harden our heart or close our mind to anyone.

It's not easy to keep this vow, of course. But every time we break it, what's important is that we recognize that we've closed someone out, that we've distanced ourselves from someone, that we've turned someone into the Other, the one on the opposite side of the fence. Often we're so full of righteous indignation, so charged up, that we don't even see that we've been triggered. But if we're fortunate, we realize what's happened—or it's pointed out to us—and we acknowledge to ourselves what we've done. Then we simply renew our commitment to stay open to others, aspiring to start fresh.

Some people like to read or recite an inspiring verse as part of renewing their commitment. One we could use is the verse from Shantideva that is traditionally repeated to reaffirm the intention to benefit others:

Just as the awakened ones of the past
Aroused an awakened mind
And progressively established themselves
In the practices of the Bodhisattva,
So I too for the benefit of beings
Shall arouse an awakened mind
And progressively train myself in those practices.

We repeat these words or something similar to renew our commitment; then it's a new moment and we go forward. We will stumble again and start again over and over, but as long as the seed is planted, we will always be moving in the direction of being more and more open to others, more and more compassionate and caring.

The commitment to take care of one another, the warrior commitment, is not about being perfect. It's about continuing to put virtuous input into our unconscious, continuing to sow the seeds that predispose our heart to expand without limit, that predispose us to awaken. Every time we recognize that we've broken this commitment, rather than criticize ourselves, rather than sow seeds of self-judgment and self-denigration—or seeds of righteous indignation, rage, or whatever other frustrations we take out on other people—we can sow seeds of strength, seeds of confidence, seeds of love and compassion. We're sowing seeds so that we will become more and more like that grandfather and the many other people we know—or have heard about— who seem to be happy to put their life on the line for the sake of others.

When you do feel bad about yourself for your rigid and unforgiving heart, you can take consolation from Shantideva. He says that when he took the vow to save all sentient beings, it was "clear insanity," because even though he was unaware of it at the time, he was "subject to the same afflictions" as others—he was as confused as anyone else.

Our confusion is the confusion that everyone feels. So when you think that you've blown it in every possible way, that you've broken the commitment irredeemably, Shantideva suggests that instead of becoming mired in guilt, you view it as an incentive to spend the rest of your life recognizing your habitual tendencies and doing your best not to strengthen them.

Making the warrior commitment is like being on a sinking ship and vowing to help all the other passengers get off the boat before we do. A few years ago, I saw a perfect example of this when a U.S. Air plane went down in the Hudson River in New York City. Shortly after the plane took off from LaGuardia Airport, birds knocked out the engines, and the pilot had no choice but to ditch the plane in the river. The landing was so skillful that all 155 people aboard the aircraft survived. I can still picture them standing on the wings until they were rescued by a flotilla of small boats that rushed to the scene. The story is that the pilot stayed on the plane until everyone was safely out, then searched it again twice to make sure that no one was left behind. That's the kind of role model who embodies the warrior commitment.

On the other hand, I've also heard stories from people who were in similar situations but fled for safety without giving a thought to anyone else. They always talk about how bad that makes them feel in retrospect. One woman told me about being in a plane crash many years ago. The passengers were ordered to evacuate right away because the plane would probably blow up. The woman raced for the exit, not stopping to help anyone, not even an old man struggling to undo his seatbelt and unable to get free. Afterward, it weighed pretty heavily on her that she hadn't stopped to help him, and it has inspired her to reach out to others as much as she can, whenever she has the chance.

Shantideva says that the only way to break this vow completely is to give up altogether on wanting to help others, not caring if we're harming them because we only want to make sure that Number One is safe and secure. We run into trouble only when we close down and couldn't care less—when we're too cynical or depressed or full of doubt even to bother.

At the heart of making this commitment is training in not fearing fundamental edginess, fundamental uneasiness, when it arises in us. Our challenge is to train in smiling at groundlessness, smiling at fear. I've had years of training in this because I get panic attacks. As anyone who has experienced a panic attack knows, that feeling of terror can arise out of nowhere. For me it often comes in the middle of the night, when I'm especially vulnerable. But over the years I've trained myself to relax into that heart-stopping, mind-stopping feeling. My first reaction is always to gasp with fright. But Chögyam Trungpa used to gasp like that when he was describing how to recognize awakened mind. So now, whenever a panic attack comes and I gasp, I picture Chögyam Trungpa's face and think of him gasping as he talked about awakened mind. Then the energy of panic passes through me.

If you resist that kind of panicky energy, even at an involuntary, unconscious level, the fear can last a long time. The way to work with it is to drop the story line and not pull back or buy into the idea, "This isn't okay," but instead to smile at the panic, smile at this dreadful, bottomless, gaping hole that's opening up in the pit of your stomach. When you can smile at fear, there's a shift: what you usually try to escape from becomes a vehicle for awakening you to your fundamental, primordial goodness, for awakening you to clear-mindedness, to a caring that holds nothing back.

The image of the warrior is of a person who can go into the worst of hells and not waver from the direct experience of cruelty and unimaginable pain. So that's our path: even in the most difficult situations, we do our best to smile at fear, to smile at our righteous indignation, our cowardliness, our avoidance of vulnerability.

Traditionally, there are three ways of entering the warrior path, three approaches to making the commitment to benefit others. The first is called entering like a monarch—like a king or a queen. This means getting our own kingdom together, then on the basis of that strength, taking care of our subjects. The analogy is, *I work on myself and get my own life together so that I benefit others. To the degree that I'm not triggered anymore, I can stay present and not close my mind and heart.* Our motivation is to be there for other people more and more as the years go by.

Parents get good training in this. Most mothers and fathers aspire to give their children a good life—one free of aggression or meanness. But then there's the reality of how infuriating children can be. There's the reality of losing your temper and yelling, the reality of being irritable, unreasonable, immature. When we see the discrepancy between our good intentions and our actions, it motivates us to work with our minds, to work with our habitual reactions and our impatience. It motivates us to get better at knowing our triggers and refraining from acting out or repressing. We gladly work on ourselves in order to be more skillful and loving parents.

People in the caring professions also get plenty of training in entering like a monarch. Maybe you want to work with homeless teenagers because you were once one yourself. Your desire is to make a difference in even one person's life, so that they can feel that someone is there for them. Then before long, you find yourself so activated by the behavior of young people that you totally lose it and can't be there for them anymore. At that point, you turn to meditation or to the first commitment to support you in being present and open to whatever presents itself, including feelings of inadequacy, incompetence, or shame.

The next way to approach the warrior commitment is with the attitude of the ferryman. We cross the river in the company of all sentient beings—we open to our true nature together. Here the analogy is, *my pain will become the stepping-stone for understanding the pain of others.* Rather than our own suffering making us more self-absorbed, it becomes the means by which we genuinely open to others' suffering.

A number of cancer survivors have told me that this attitude is what gave them the strength to go through the physical and psychological misery of chemotherapy. They couldn't eat or drink because everything hurt too much. They had sores in their mouths. They were dehydrated. They had tremendous nausea. Then they received instruction in tonglen. Their world got bigger and bigger as they opened to all the other people who were experiencing the same physical pain that they were, as well as the loneliness, anger, and other emotional distress that goes along with it. Their pain became a stepping-stone to understanding the distress of others in the same boat.

I remember one woman telling me, "It couldn't have gotten any worse, so I had no problem breathing in and saying, 'Since the pain is here anyway, may I take it in fully and completely with the wish that nobody else will have to feel like this.' And I had no problem sending out relief." It's not as if your nausea goes away, she said. It's not as if you can suddenly eat and drink. But the practice gives meaning to your suffering. Your attitude shifts. The feeling of resistance to the pain, the feeling of utter helplessness, and the feeling of hopelessness disappear.

There's no way to make a dreadful situation pretty. But we can use the pain of it to recognize our sameness with other people. Shantideva said that since all sentient beings suffer from strong, conflicting emotions, and all sentient beings get what they don't want and can't hold on to what they do want, and all sentient beings have physical distress, why am I making such a big deal about just me? Since we're all in this together, why am I making such a big deal about myself? The attitude of the ferryman is that whatever usually drags us down and causes us to withdraw into ourselves is the stepping-stone for awakening our compassion and for contacting the vast, unbiased mind of the warrior.

The third attitude is that of the shepherd and shepherdess, whose flock always comes first. This is the grandfather with the frogs or the pilot of the sinking plane. It's the story of firemen entering a burning building or a father risking his life to save his child. The shepherd and shepherdess automatically put others before themselves.

Almost everyone assumes that putting others first is how we're always supposed to approach the warrior commitment. And if we do anything less, we criticize ourselves. But one way of entry isn't better than another. It could be said that we evolve toward the attitude of the shepherd and shepherdess, but it's a natural evolution. The other two approaches are no less valid. The importance of this teaching is to point out that all three approaches are admirable, beautiful, to-be-applauded ways of making the warrior commitment.

In fact, most of us use all three approaches. There are probably many examples in your life of working on yourself with the aspiration to be present and useful to other people. And there are times when your sorrow has connected you with the sorrow of others, when your grief or physical pain has been a catalyst for appreciating what another person is going through. There are also times when you spontaneously put others first.

Coldheartedness and narrow-mindedness are not the kinds of habits we want to reinforce. They won't predispose us to awakening—in fact, they will keep us stuck. So we make the warrior commitment—take the vow to care for one another—then do our best to never turn our backs on anyone. And when we falter, we renew our commitment and move on, knowing that even the awakened ones of the past understood what it felt like to relapse. Otherwise, how could they have any idea about what other beings go through? Otherwise, how could they have cultivated patience and forgiveness, loving-kindness and compassion?

The Third Commitment
Committing to Embrace the World Just as It Is

Chaos should be regarded as extremely good news.

—CHÖGYAM TRUNGPA RINPOCHE

9

Nowhere to Hide

WITH THE THIRD COMMITMENT, we step fully into groundlessness, relaxing into the continually changing nature of our situation and experiencing it as awakened energy, as the manifestation of basic goodness. In some sense, this is nothing new. It's what we've been training in all along. But experientially it's a big leap forward, and it points us toward a major shift in consciousness. We take what we've integrated from the previous commitments, particularly being fully present with an open heart, and up the ante. Here the emphasis is on *fully,* and the demand to put *fully present* into practice is far greater. This definitely squeezes the old self-absorbed habit of ego clinging considerably. The feeling of nowhere to hide can be quite intense.

Once, when I had spent several months devoting myself as continuously as I could to this practice, I complained to Chögyam Trungpa that I felt as if I would jump out of my skin. I was irritated by even specks of dust and ready to snap at people all the time. He replied that this was because the practice was demanding that I be sane, demanding that I grow up, and I wasn't used to that yet.

The third commitment, traditionally known as the Samaya Vow, is a commitment to embrace the world just as it is. *Samaya* is a Tibetan word meaning "sacred vow" or "binding vow." It entails a coming together with our total experience, an unshakable bond with life. With this commitment, we accept that we are bound to reality, bound to everything we perceive in every moment. There is no way to get away from our experience, nowhere to go other than right where we are. We surrender to life. We give in and settle down with all the sights, sounds, smells, tastes, thoughts, and people we encounter. This is a commitment to not reject anything. The words of the Tibetan Buddhist master Dilgo Khyentse express this beautifully:

> The everyday practice is simply to develop a complete acceptance and openness to all situations and emotions, and to all people, experiencing everything totally without mental reservations and blockages, so that one never withdraws or centralizes into oneself.

The attitude of the third commitment is that we live in a world that is intrinsically good, intrinsically awake, and our path is to realize this. Simply put, the practice at this stage is to turn toward your experience, all of it, and never turn away.

First, you continue to live by the other commitments. You practice mindfulness, coming back over and over to exactly where you are and what you're experiencing: feet on the floor, knee hurting, warm water flowing over your hands, winter air stinging your eyes, sound of hammering, smell of coffee.

Then you add to that a sense of deep appreciation for each of those unique and precious moments. You may wish the workmen would stop hammering—it's been going on all day, every day, for a month, and you're fed up with it. But it will pass. And when you look back a year later, it will seem as if the hammering were over in a finger snap. Hearing the hammering is a fleeting, transitory experience, and each time the hammer hits is a unique moment. You will never hear sound exactly like that again.

No matter how irritated you are by what you're hearing, each sound is worthy of your attention. When you listen to it with appreciation, it begins to draw you out of yourself, out of the small, self-centered world that is always just about Me. When you have this kind of genuine connection with yourself and the world, you may begin to encounter wakefulness. You suddenly feel as if you're in a vast, wide-open space with unlimited breathing room. It's as if you've stepped out of a small, dark, stuffy tent and found yourself standing on the rim of the Grand Canyon. This is the place of just being. It's not an otherworldly, ethereal place. You haven't transcended the ordinary details of your life. Quite the opposite. You've finally contacted them 100 percent, and they've become a doorway to what in the Vajrayana tradition is called sacred world. Sacred not in the sense of religious or holy but in the sense of precious, rare, fleeting, fundamentally genuine and good.

There are some verses by Chögyam Trungpa that describe what such a world is like. He begins by describing sight as a doorway to sacred world:

Whatever is seen with the eyes is vividly unreal in emptiness, yet there is still form.

"Vividly unreal in emptiness" refers to the ordinary, everyday world, empty of concept, free of labels, clearly perceived in all of its brilliance but never fully graspable. Then the verse goes on to say "yet there is still form." Emptiness and form are forever inseparable. What we see—our perception of ordinary, no-big-deal sights—is the form, the manifestation of emptiness, of awakened energy. From the moment we wake up in the morning to the moment we fall asleep—and even in our dreams—there is continuous, ceaseless manifestation. We always have the opportunity to let our sight connect us with the preciousness of this sacred world.

Emptiness is not a void, a blank space where nothing is happening. The whole point is that discovering basic goodness—discovering the awakeness, the is-ness, the nowness of things—doesn't happen by transcending ordinary reality. It comes from appreciating simple experiences free of story line. When we see a red car with a dented door; when we feel heat or cold, softness or hardness; when we taste a plum or smell rotting leaves, these simple, direct experiences are our contact with basic wakefulness, with basic goodness, with sacred world. It's only by fully touching our relative experience that we discover the fresh, timeless, ultimate nature of our world.

Once in the early seventies, a student stood up at a talk and demanded that Chögyam Trungpa tell him what enlightenment is. I've always remembered his answer. "Enlightenment," he said, "is like hearing a bugle or smelling tobacco for the first time." That is the viewpoint behind this teaching on the third commitment. If we hide from our experience or dismiss it as insignificant, we are losing a chance for enlightenment.

Continuing, the verse says,

Whatever is heard with the ears is the echo of emptiness, yet real.

Hearing, along with our other perceptions, is also a doorway to sacred world. Whatever we hear is the echo, the sound, of emptiness, of awakened energy, ungraspable yet audible. It's also "the clear and distinct utterance of the guru"—the voice of the teacher. If someone is talking to us, even when we don't like what they're saying, that's not just some ordinary schmuck nattering on. It's the voice of the teacher, the sound of emptiness, of awakened energy manifesting. If a raven outside our window is piercing our eardrums with its raucous cry, that's the sound of awakened energy, the voice of the teacher waking us up.

There is nothing we can see or hear that isn't a manifestation of enlightened energy, that isn't a doorway to sacred world. This is the view of the third commitment. It's the view we commit to when we vow to embrace the world just as it is. We vow to appreciate ourselves and our world. We vow to turn toward and never turn away.

Ordinarily, we are constantly projecting our preferences onto whatever is manifesting. Everything comes with our mixed feelings—our personal preferences, our cultural baggage—as well as with *plenty* of shenpa. But as Chögyam Trungpa said, "It's like saying 'oatmeal.' Some people like hot cereal and some people hate it. Nevertheless, oatmeal remains oatmeal."

If we look at the snow outside our window in winter, we can see its color, how it falls, how it accumulates on the ground and on cars and on tree branches, how it forms piles of different shapes. We can see its crystals sparkling in sunlight and the blue-white of its shadows. We can see snow as snow, without adding anything extra. But usually we don't see snow that way. Our vision is clouded by our

emotional reactions. We like it, or we don't like it. It makes us happy, or it makes us sad. It makes us anxious or irritated, because we have to shovel it before we go to work and we're already running late.

Even with mixed feelings, there are degrees of intensity. We can like the snow with clinging, with shenpa ("I really hope it sticks so we can ski this weekend"), but we can also like it without clinging, without shenpa. We can *not* like it with shenpa, with righteous indignation ("How dare it snow on the day of my big party"), but we can also *not* like it without shenpa, without any emotional attachment. But regardless of how we feel about snow, it's still snow—awakened energy manifesting, just as it is. It's possible to see it without a story line.

Chögyam Trungpa's verses go on to say,

> Good or bad, happy or sad, all thoughts vanish into
> emptiness like the imprint of a bird in the sky.

Whatever occurs in your mind—thoughts about getting revenge or how to cheat on your taxes or what you're planning to do when this meeting is over; spiritual thoughts, aggressive thoughts, anxious thoughts, cheerful thoughts—whatever occurs is the manifestation of emptiness, the manifestation of enlightened mind. The path to unshakable well-being lies in being completely present and open to all sights, all sounds, all thoughts—never withdrawing, never hiding, never needing to jazz them up or tone them down.

This is a tricky idea to grasp, no question. That's why we train in the first two commitments, with the building blocks of refraining from harming with our speech or actions and not closing our mind and heart to anyone. We need that

deep training to reach the place where everything becomes the path of awakening.

Much of the training in the first two commitments involves minimizing our tendency to pin our labels and preconceptions, our views and opinions, on everything we perceive. With the third commitment, we take that still further. It's not that we can't have views and opinions about oatmeal or snow—or anything else, for that matter. It's just that we don't cling to those views. Instead, we try them on, have fun with them, like an actor or actress in a play. We can dance with life when it's a wild party completely out of control, and we can dance with life when it's as tender as a lover. We work with whatever we have, with whoever we are, right now.

This commitment is about engaging with the simplicity of life, with life just as it comes, without frills. We begin to see our views and opinions—even the ones that have a lot of heat in them—as no more, no less than our views and opinions. Snow remains snow. Oatmeal remains oatmeal, whether we want it never to be on the menu for the rest of time or we love it so much that we open a health spa where it's on the menu at every meal.

Consider another example: smoking. Some people think smoking is bad, the worst thing on the planet. Some people love smoking and feel abused by all the restrictions that are being imposed on them. Nevertheless, smoking remains smoking. You may be reading this and thinking that you're not sure you buy this perspective—everyone *knows* cigarette smoking is a health hazard, and look, here's a 570-page study on lung cancer and the effects of secondhand smoke. But consider the vehemence with which you oppose the idea that smoking is just smoking or the vehemence with which you support it. Smoking may not be intrinsically right or wrong, but it certainly stirs up a lot of shenpa.

All the wars, all the hatred, all the ignorance in the world come out of being so invested in our opinions. And at bottom, those opinions are merely our efforts to escape the underlying uneasiness of being human, the uneasiness of feeling like we can't get ground under our feet. So we hold on to our fixed ideas of *this is how it is* and disparage any opposing views. But imagine what the world would be like if we could come to see our likes and dislikes as merely likes and dislikes, and what we take to be intrinsically true as just our personal viewpoint.

The third commitment is not future oriented. It's about being fully open to whatever is coming along right now. It involves leaning in to our direct experience, appreciating our direct experience, being one with our direct experience, not coloring our sense perceptions with our concepts, our internal dialogue, our interpretations of what's going on. When we feel uneasy, we tend to become very opinionated and cling to our views, trying to get rid of that shaky, edgy feeling. But another way to deal with that uneasy feeling would be to stay present with it and renew our commitment to sanity. This vow requires deep training in bearing witness to ourselves with immense compassion. We bear witness to ourselves when we pull back into fixed ideas, into fixed identity and ego clinging, into wanting life on our terms—all in order to escape the fundamental ambiguity of being human. With the third commitment, we come to know ourselves with kindness and immense honesty. This is going deeper with making friends with ourselves.

With the commitment to embrace the world, we continue to question our belief in a fixed identity. In a poem written just before his death, the Chan master Sheng Yen wrote, "Intrinsically, there's no I. Life and Death thus cast aside." At the end of life, it becomes clear that there's no fixed identity, that in terms of this particular body, this particular identity, we're going to leave it behind. But that begs the question: If there's no intrinsic I, then who feels all this pleasure and pain? Master Sheng's death poem went on to say, "Within emptiness, smiling, weeping." He didn't say, "Within emptiness, not engaging in life."

But it's only when the fearful "I" is not pushing and pulling at life, freaking out and grasping at it, that full engagement is possible. We become more fully engaged in our lives when we become less self-absorbed. As we have less and less allegiance to our small, egocentric self, less and less allegiance to a fixed notion of who we are or what we're capable of doing, we find we also have less and less fear of embracing the world just as it is. As Leonard Cohen once said about the benefits of many years of meditation, "The less there was of me, the happier I got."

Letting go of the fixed self isn't something we can just *wish* to happen, however. It's something we predispose ourselves to with every gesture, every word, every deed, every thought. We're either going in the direction of letting go and strengthening that ability or going in the direction of holding on and reinforcing that fear-based habit. We can choose reality—stay with it, be here, show up, be open, turn toward the sights and the sounds and the thoughts that pass through our minds—or we can choose to turn away. But if we turn away, we can pretty much count on staying stuck in the same old pattern of suffering, never getting closer to experiencing wakefulness, never getting closer to experiencing the sacredness of our existence.

The Tibetan teacher Anam Thubten once gave a talk entitled "Falling in Love with Emptiness." That captures the feeling of the third commitment: falling in love with the human condition and not dividing ourselves in two, with the so-called good part condemning the so-called bad part and the bad part scheming to undermine the good part. We're not trying to cultivate one part of ourselves and get rid of another part. We're training in opening to it all.

In his talk, Anam Thubten said that in order to fall in love with emptiness, we have to ask ourselves an important question: "Am I willing to let go of everything?" In other words, am I willing to let go of anything that is a barrier between me and others, a barrier between me and the world? This is what you need to ask yourself before you can unequivocally make a commitment to embrace the world. But there's no need to be hard on yourself if your answer is unequivocally "yes" one day and "this is too difficult" the next. Keeping this commitment is traditionally said to be like keeping dust from settling on a mirror. Just as with the warrior's vow, this vow is easily broken, but we can mend it by simply recommitting to staying open to life.

Each person's life is like a mandala—a vast, limitless circle. We stand in the center of our own circle, and everything we see, hear, and think forms the mandala of our life. We enter a room, and the room is our mandala. We get on the subway, and the subway car is our mandala, down to the teenager checking messages on her iPhone and the homeless man slumped in the corner. We go for a hike in the mountains, and everything as far as we can see is our mandala: the clouds, the trees, the snow on the peaks, even the rattlesnake coiled on the path. We're lying in a hospital bed, and the hospital is our mandala. We don't set it up; we don't get to choose what or who shows up in it. It is, as Chögyam Trungpa said, "the mandala that is never arranged but is always complete." And we embrace it just as it is.

Everything that shows up in your mandala is a vehicle for your awakening. From this point of view, awakening is right at your fingertips continually. There's not a drop of rain or a pile of dog poop that appears in your life that isn't the manifestation of enlightened energy, that isn't a doorway to sacred world. But it's up to you whether your life is a mandala of neurosis or a mandala of sanity.

The pain of your confused mind and the brilliance of your awakened mind make up the mandala of your life. It's an environment in which birth and death, depression and joy, can coexist. No problem. The beauty, the kindness, the nobility, the excellence, the heartbreak, the cruelty, the ignorance—you can embrace it all. You don't need to avoid any of it. Even difficult emotions like anger, craving, ignorance, jealousy, and pride are part of your mandala, and you can welcome them.

Whatever appears in our nighttime dreams, whatever appears in our waking life—in our mandala—is vividly unreal, and yet that's all there is. We can call it poison; we can call it wisdom. Either way, it's up to us whether we work with it or try to run away. The third commitment invites us to make the mandala of our life an ally and the birthplace of our enlightenment.

The Zen master Dogen said, "To know the self is to forget the self. To forget the self is to be enlightened by all things." The only way to forget the self—to realize that there is no fixed, intrinsic self—is to know the self. We have to know ourselves fully and completely, avoiding nothing, never averting our gaze. We have to be curious about this thing called My Life, curious about this person called Me. With the commitment to embrace the world, we move in close and investigate.

The last words of Dogen's teaching say, "To forget the self is to be enlightened by all things." With this commitment we vow to not get in our own way, we vow to stop insisting that things be the way we want them to be and to stop insisting that the way we want them to be is the way they really are. To forget the self, we first have to know our shenpa, our propensities, our exits really well—and then be willing to let them go. We have to be willing to overcome the laziness that keeps us biting the same hooks again and again as if it didn't matter. We have to be willing to listen to our wisdom instead of following our robotic, habitual patterns. We have to be willing to invite scary feelings to stay longer so that we can get to know them to their depth. We have to be willing to entertain the thought that we are basically sane, basically good, and that we have the potential to be fully and utterly awake.

Then, when we're no longer seduced by the self, Dogen says we will be enlightened by all things. That's the third-commitment experience: life as an enlightened mandala that is always encouraging us to be awake, to be alive, to be fully present, to be more accommodating and more available to others.

The commitment to not cause harm is very specific about what we're to cultivate and what we're to refrain from. There's a list of so-called virtuous actions and a list of so-called nonvirtuous actions. We don't lie; instead we're truthful. We don't steal; instead we're generous. And so on. But with the third commitment, we have to find out for ourselves how to proceed. There are no instructions. There is nothing to hold on to. You have to decide for yourself what gives you inner strength, what minimizes your confusion, what helps you get unstuck, what brings you closer to experiencing life without a story line. And then you refrain from anything that is too overwhelming at present—anything you're not ready to deal with yet. But always your aspiration is to reach the point where there's nothing you can't deal with, nothing you can't work with. Until then, you simply move in the direction of clarity, becoming more and more able to see shenpa as shenpa, being hooked as being hooked, views and opinions as just views and opinions.

The key to this commitment is to be honest with yourself about what you can and can't handle at the moment. If you're trying to recover from drug abuse, for example, you don't hang out with your old drug dealer. If you're trying to recover from alcoholism, you don't hang out in bars. But with the third commitment, unlike the first commitment, there's no list of dos and don'ts, nothing that says "don't go to bars." Whatever list there may be is your own list—a list that is merely an indication of where you are at present. You're not looking to avoid these things for the rest of your life. If you're a recovering alcoholic, for instance, you would probably like to reach the point where your recovery is so dependable that you can help people who are still caught in the addictive cycle. In order to do that, you might, on occasion, find yourself in a bar. But if after twenty minutes in the bar you say to yourself, "To really be of help to this person, I think I should have just one little drink," then you're only kidding yourself.

We have to decide matters like that for ourselves. At the level of the third commitment, decisions are personal, individual. We might wish there were a list telling us what we should and shouldn't do, but there isn't. The responsibility falls on us.

Together, the Three Commitments form the education of the warrior. On the warrior path, we train patiently in never turning away from our experience. And when we do turn away, it's based on being able to discriminate between turning away because we know we can't handle something at the moment and turning away because we don't want to feel what we're feeling, don't want to feel our vulnerability. But we don't develop this discrimination all at once. We get there inch by inch, moment by moment, step by step, working with our mind and heart.

People often ask me, "How do we know whether to refrain from something or go toward it?" My answer is, just practice what comes naturally at the time. If the first commitment, refraining, seems like it would be the most helpful, do that. But if you feel that you can keep your heart and mind open a little longer to someone who's irritating you or triggering your impatience, then follow your instinct and do that. Then maybe, based on having been able to stay open a little longer in that situation, you'll begin to get a sense of what it would mean to not turn away at all.

As we go deeper with our experience, we begin to be able to speak and act freely, fully confident that we won't cause harm. But without self-awareness—without knowing whether we're hooked, knowing whether our heart and mind are open or closed—we're almost sure to create confusion and pain. Our intention with this vow is to open completely to whatever arises, to experience exactly where we are as sacred ground. A confused mind perceives the world as confused. But the unfixated mind perceives the world as a pure land, a mandala of awakening.

What's happening on our earth today is the result of the collective minds of everyone on the planet. So the message is that each of us has to take responsibility for our own state of mind. The third commitment points to how the world could be transformed from a place of escalating aggression, with everyone defending their territory and their fixed ideas, to a place of awakening.

If our minds become cold and cruel and capable of harming others without a second thought, war erupts and the environment deteriorates. Even the most brilliant political system can't save the world if the people are still committed to a fear-based way of living. Peace and prosperity come from how we, the citizens of the world, are working with our minds. By not running from the vicissitudes of life, by fearlessly opening to them all, we have the opportunity not only to change our own life but also to help change the earth.

I think it's important to emphasize that we work on the mind and then, based on that, take action. And we take action with the understanding that everyone is basically good. No one is cast out. No one is excommunicated from the mandala. When the conditions come together, even people whose lives have not been exemplary can rise to the occasion and help others. Think of Oskar Schindler, the German industrialist who saved hundreds of Jews in World War II by employing them in his munitions and metalwork factories. He wasn't the nicest guy on the planet: to many, he was a profiteer who partied with the SS elite. Yet Schindler doggedly defended his workers against Nazi efforts to deport them, and he will always be remembered for his nobility and courage.

Like Schindler, most of us are a rich mixture of rough

and smooth, bitter and sweet. But wherever we are right now, whatever our lives are like in the moment, this is our mandala, our working basis for awakening. The awakened life isn't somewhere else—in some distant place that's accessible only when we've got it all together. With the commitment to embrace the world just as it is, we begin to see that sanity and goodness are always present and can be uncovered right here, right now.

10

Awakening in the Charnel Ground

In Tibet, because the ground is frozen most of the year, earth burial is impossible. So when someone dies, the body is cut into pieces and taken to the charnel ground, the burial ground, where jackals and vultures and other birds of prey come and feed on the body parts. Strewn with limbs and eyeballs and entrails, the charnel ground is a grizzly place—hardly somewhere we would want to hang out.

But it's in just such a place, surrounded by vivid reminders of death and impermanence, that brave meditators can practice staying awake and present under the most difficult circumstances. It's right there in the midst of such intensity that we can train most deeply in keeping the commitment to embrace the world.

The charnel ground has become a metaphor for life exactly as it is rather than how we would like it to be. In this basic ground, many kinds of experiences coexist simultaneously. Uncertainty and unpredictability, impermanence and change, good times and hard times, sorrow and joy, loss and gain—all of this constitutes our home ground, the mandala of our life, our base for practicing fearlessness and compassion. This is our potential richness, our power. So we work with it rather than struggle against it. If we aspire to find freedom exactly where we are, there could be no more fertile ground for our awakening.

Charnel-ground practice tests our commitment to embrace the world. It expands the range of "just as it is" far beyond what we find comfortable. This is a practice for facing the fullness of our life, not hiding the unacceptable, embarrassing, disagreeable parts; not favoring one kind of experience over another; not rejecting our experience when it hurts or clinging to it when it's going our way. In the charnel ground, we meet both wretchedness and splendidness—the totality of our experience as human beings—and discover that we need both to be a genuine warrior. The splendidness of life lifts our spirits, and we go forward with enthusiasm. When we hear pleasant news or meet with inspiring teachers, when we enjoy the company of good friends or find ourselves in beautiful places, when we feel that everything is ideal and hunky-dory, then naturally we feel joyful and at ease. But should all of this good fortune make us arrogant or complacent or indifferent to the suffering of others, wretchedness humbles us. It cuts through any sense of superiority or entitlement, through any delusions that comfort is somehow our birthright. On the other hand, if there is too much wretchedness—too much misery and despair—it makes us want to collapse and never get out of bed. So the sweetness of life and the harshness of life complement each other. Splendidness provides vision, and wretchedness grounds us. Just when we're ready to give up, a kind word or the sight of the ocean or the sound of beautiful music can save the day. Just when we're riding high and becoming arrogant, a sudden misfortune or bad news from the doctor or the unexpected death of a loved one can abruptly bring us down to earth and reconnect us with our tender heart.

When life is uncomfortable, when we're highly agitated

and don't know where to turn, that's the most difficult time to stay present. But that's also the time when doing so can be the most rewarding. It's a challenge to practice staying present when we're despondent or distressed or overwhelmed, when our backs are against the wall. But right then, when we're in a tight spot, we have the ideal situation for practice. We can do something radical: accept suffering as part of our home ground, part of our enlightened mandala, and relate to it straightforwardly. We don't awaken in some paradise where the circumstances are made to order. We awaken in the charnel ground.

So when you find yourself in a situation that is bound to trigger your propensities—spending extended time with your relatives would be an excellent example—you can practice holding your seat and relating fully to exactly where you are. If you can stay present in even the most challenging circumstances, the intensity of the situation will transform you. When you can see even the worst of hells as a place where you can awaken, your world will change dramatically.

This isn't how we usually relate to difficulties and discomfort, of course. There are those fortunate few who seem to consider everything an adventure, no matter how challenging or painful it is, but most of us don't view life that way. And if someone suggests that our suffering is a great opportunity for practice, we're not likely to take it kindly. It's built into our DNA that when things are unpleasant and fearful, we look for the nearest exit. If we find ourselves in a burning building, we instinctively head for the door. Wanting to escape pain is the reason that many people start on a spiritual path. It can be a good motivator, because it drives us to look for answers. The problem is, most of us spend our entire life going from one promise of relief to another, never staying with the pain long enough to learn anything from it.

But sooner or later, we all encounter intense emotion that we can't outrun. It may be fear that arises in a truly disturbing situation or the feeling of being very hooked and about to be swept away. One sign that you've already started charnel-ground practice, whether you realize it or not, is if you perk up when strong feelings come along and then, instead of trying to get rid of them, you move toward them and get curious. When you're open to inviting difficult emotions to stick around long enough to teach you something, then you're already in the frame of mind to do this practice.

Whatever we've understood and internalized from dedicating ourselves to the first two commitments serves as the foundation for charnel-ground practice. Without that base, working with such intense feelings would be overwhelming. With the commitment to not cause harm, we learn to acknowledge shenpa when it arises and to refrain from acting and speaking out of our confusion. We begin to train in staying present and increasing our tolerance for groundlessness. With the second commitment, we go a step further and train in being fully aware of our feelings, and with that as our base, extend ourselves to others. We begin to sense deeply our sameness with all beings, animals and people alike, and to feel their struggles as our own. As we start to untangle ourselves from confusion and pain, we long to help others untangle themselves as well. This is a far more daring, less cozy way to live, and it puts us squarely in touch with the groundlessness of our condition.

Having begun to establish a more compassionate and

honest relationship with the world, we can go further still and overcome any remaining hesitation about dealing with the ugliness of life. With the third commitment, we don't reject anything that turns up in our mandala of awakening. In fact, we feel quite sympathetic toward the unkempt quality of life. Right in the middle of this fertile ground, with the jackals and vultures looming over us, we take our seat and begin to practice. We begin with the understanding that we can't experience profound well-being without working with, not against, the gritty reality of life.

A soldier with post-traumatic stress disorder told me that this radically different approach to pain had saved his life. He had finally found a way to work with his recurring flashbacks of seeing a comrade he was very close to being blown to pieces right beside him. Instead of trying to get rid of the horrific memories and the emotions they triggered, he had been encouraged by a therapist to turn toward them, to lean into his emotions and feel them as bravely as he could. Doing this in short sessions had allowed him to relax with his vulnerability and helplessness and with the feeling that his friend's death had been his fault, that he could have prevented it, and that he didn't deserve to be the one who survived. Little by little, as he let the feelings arise, build in intensity, and pass away, his overwhelming sense of guilt and failure began to lighten up, and for the first time in three years, he was able to sleep through the night.

When I first started to approach life with a more warrior-like spirit, I was dying for something to go wrong so I would have something really juicy to work with. But I soon discovered that as keen as I was for my propensities to arise so that I could free myself from them, when it happened—when the dog got its teeth in my arm—it was very humbling. I felt deep compassion for what we're up against as human beings. If we're doing this practice in earnest, the emotions and habitual patterns we're working with can hit us with such force that it takes everything in us not to run.

Sometimes I felt like Odysseus, lashed to the mast so I wouldn't follow the Sirens' song. It was as if a giant magnet were trying to drag me away from staying present. I would just begin to sit with an intense feeling when a little voice in my head would start saying things like "You'd better check to see if you turned off the stove" and "Maybe this is bad for your heart." Our old habits are worthy opponents. Even if we're eager to have everything fall apart so we can do charnel-ground practice, when we actually do it, it puts us through a lot. We need strong motivation to stick with it because the desire to escape is so compelling.

From the perspective of charnel-ground practice, the chaos in our lives isn't terrible. It's simply the material we work with. Viscerally, however, it *feels* terrible, and we don't like it a bit. So it takes courage and gentle, compassionate discipline just to hold our seat. What keeps us moving forward is that the practice puts us in touch with the living energy of our emotions—an energy that has tremendous power, the power to wake us up. Because of its intensity, it can pop us out of our neurosis, pop us out of our fearful cocoon, pop us into sacred world.

When I talk about awakening in the charnel ground, I'm not referring to any traditional form of practice but, rather, to the essence of the practice. To me this is epitomized by one of Dzigar Kongtrül's teachings:

Feel your emotions directly and selflessly, and let their power open you up.

For some time now, I've been working with that as a basic practice instruction, exploring those words as a support for relating to unwanted feelings and a way to move beyond small-mindedness, complacency, and the self-serving bubble of ego, a way to step further into groundlessness.

Ordinarily, uncomfortable emotions don't open us, they close us down. We become more fearful. The mind goes crazy, concocting elaborate scenarios and trying to figure out how to get rid of those unsettling, disagreeable feelings. Our main strategy is usually to blame others for how we feel. Because we tend to project so much onto the outer situation, Dzigar Kongtrül's instruction is to cut through our habitual reactions and feel the emotions *directly. Directly* means without commentary, without interpretation, without having a conversation in your head about what's happening. It means not regarding the emotions as adversaries but joining with them, embracing them, becoming intimate with them. If thoughts arise, the instruction is to interrupt their momentum by letting them go, then to touch in again with the rawness of the energy. Experiencing the rawness of emotion directly is like accidentally putting your hand on a hot burner and feeling the pain as pure sensation, without embellishment.

When you touch a hot stove, as soon as you become aware of the pain, you immediately pull your hand away. You don't let it rest on the burner in order to explore the pain. In the same way, in charnel-ground practice, we stay present with strong emotion only very briefly at first. The instruction is: *short moments again and again.* Rather than trying to endure prolonged exposure to intense feeling, we touch in for only two or three seconds, then pause and breathe gently before touching in again. Or we might simply stay with the troubling feeling for five or six minutes and then go on with our day, more in touch with our emotions and, therefore, less likely to be dragged around by them.

Practicing in the charnel ground is like taking small sips of a bitter medicine over time rather than drinking the entire bottle at once. Gradually, sip by sip, bit by bit, we create the conditions for staying present with whatever is happening in our body and mind. We cultivate new ways of viewing our experience, new ways of dealing with discomfort, new ways of embracing groundlessness. The soldier with PTSD told me that the instruction to do the practice in small bites was crucial in enabling him to stay present.

Charnel-ground practice as I'm describing it is usually done on the spot wherever you are, with whatever is going on in the moment. *Let their power open you up,* the instructions say. Let the power of your emotions open you up. Take your seat in the middle of your home ground and rouse your confidence—your innate capacity to open to your experience. Just as in the three-step practice, you come fully into the present moment and become aware of what you're feeling physically, aware of what you're feeling mentally. You have a sense of being completely here. Then you extend warmth to your internal situation—your feelings, your state of mind—as well as to your outer situation. You meet whatever is going on with curiosity and compassion, not distancing yourself from what's happening, not having a bias about what's happening, not doing anything to escalate or exaggerate the situation. Just opening to it as fully and genuinely as you can.

But how, exactly, do we open fully? That's a question I'm often asked. *Open* means something different to everyone, so each of us has to find his or her own way of going about it. One way to experience the feeling of opening is to pay attention to your sense perceptions. Just pause and listen. Listen attentively for a few moments to sounds nearby. Listen attentively for a few moments to sounds in the distance. Listen without describing the experience to yourself or trying to figure out what you're hearing. Another way you can open to sound is to go for a walk and let hearing be the primary sensation.

You can try this same exercise with taste. Close your eyes and have someone put something to eat in your mouth without telling you what it is. See if you can experience the first taste without any preconceptions. If only for a moment, see if you can have a fresh, unconditioned experience of taste as taste, nothing extra.

You can do this practice with any sense perception. With your eyes closed, have someone take you for a short walk and then position you directly in front of an object. Open your eyes and look at the object. Look at it as if for the first time. Or the last time. If you knew you were going to die in a few minutes, you would automatically be very open, very receptive, to everything that happened in those minutes— the sights, the sounds, the feelings of your final moments.

Dzigar Kongtrül's instruction also tells us to relate to our feelings "selflessly." What does it mean to experience feelings selflessly? It means to experience them without solidifying them, without concretizing them, without clinging to them as *my* feelings, without projecting our interpretations onto them. It means to experience them without our personal trip. "Directly" is something we can train in, but "selflessly" dawns on us slowly over time. We can't force it. To me, feeling emotions selflessly happens organically, naturally, as a result of giving them our full attention free of story line. Emotion then becomes the doorway to egolessness—the doorway to experiencing the impermanence of a fixed self, the elusiveness of a fixed self, the questionableness of an unchanging, reliable "me."

We discover selflessness gradually, but always the prerequuisite is being present. When we can be present with an emotion without any distractions, we find out very quickly how insubstantial, how fleeting it is. What seemed so threatening, so solid, so lasting, begins to dissolve, giving us an immediate experience of impermanence, as the feelings arise, dwell, and then pass away. We feel an emotion and it threatens to take us over, but if we stay open to it and look directly at it, it either disappears altogether or morphs into something else. Fear might become sadness. Anger might become hopelessness. Joy might become vulnerability. When emotions start to pass away, we never know what they will become.

From staying present with impermanence and change, we become more confident, more fearless, more accepting of the groundlessness of the human condition. Our experience of selflessness deepens. If we're brave enough to experience our emotions directly and egolessly, they lose their seductiveness. The Buddhist teacher Dipa Ma gave this instruction on relating to emotions selflessly: "When you feel happy, don't get involved with the happiness. When you feel sad, don't get involved with the sadness." She went on to say, "Just be aware of them."

When you're no longer so entangled in your emotions, then you can experience their power directly. Their intensity, their dynamic energy, rather than scaring you, wakes you up. You don't discover this by trying to transcend the bitterness of life. You discover it by taking your place in the charnel ground with the confidence that this is where you belong. This is your home ground. This is where you wake up. With charnel-ground practice, you don't hold back. In the process, you develop an appetite for wakefulness.

The basic form of charnel-ground practice is familiar. It's essentially the same as the three-step practice. The difference is that in charnel-ground practice, what you're working with, what you're opening to, is far more challenging, far more intense. When you find yourself desperately wanting not to feel what you're feeling, it's probably time to do this practice.

Begin by coming fully into the present. Then, standing or sitting, take your place joyfully, fearlessly, and confidently in the midst of the chaos and pain of your life.

Feel your heart and sense that this unpleasant place is workable, that sanity exists here. Allow yourself to soften and become tender, more approachable, and more inquisitive.

Then take a leap into the next moment, "suddenly free from fixed mind," as Chögyam Trungpa put it. Go forward with compassion and an open mind.

When you do charnel-ground practice for even a few seconds, something within you starts to shift. Turning toward the intensity of life and welcoming it not only gives you a direct experience of impermanence and death and selflessness, it also gives you an appreciation for the groundlessness of life, for life as it really is.

I know prison inmates who train in charnel-ground

practice every day. In that environment, fear of death is very real. One inmate told me that for almost a year he was afraid to go out on the yard because there were inmates who wanted to kill him. But then he came face-to-face with his fear and sat with it over and over in his cell. As a result, he felt as if a load had been lifted, and now he could just be open to whatever was going on with the other men and with himself. He could go out on the yard and sit down next to someone and say, "What's happening with your life?" And the men would tell him how bad it was for them. His life began to feel like a paradise compared with what it was like for so many of the inmates. "We all die anyway," he told me, "so I'm more interested in appreciating my life and helping however I can than in staying in my cell out of fear of losing my life."

Only by completely, directly touching the reality of what's going on inside us can we embrace the bitterness, the ruggedness, the fundamental groundlessness of life as readily as we embrace the sweetness. But when the outer situation is as unstable as it is today—financial insecurity, political unrest, joblessness, homelessness, escalating wars and chaos—it's very hard to do this. So how do we keep our compassion and kindness in the middle of all of this turmoil? We turn toward it with a different attitude. Every day is an opportunity to practice in the charnel ground.

Whether we're irritated because someone took our parking place or we're overwhelmed by illness, debt, or flashbacks, it's all an opportunity to wake up. The intensity of life nowadays is triggering high levels of anxiety and inner unrest, creating the ideal environment for charnel-ground practice. We can do it in small bites throughout the day, with the attitude that we're standing confidently in the center of our life and taking it as our training ground. This is the time and this is the place where we can enter sacred world.

It's crucial for all of us to find a practice that will help us have a direct relationship with groundlessness, with impermanence and death—a practice that will enable us to touch in with the transitoriness of our thoughts, our emotions, our car, our shoes, the paint job on our house. We can get used to the fleeting quality of life in a natural, gentle, even joyful way, by watching the seasons change, watching day turning to night, watching children grow up, watching sand castles dissolve back into the sea. But if we don't find some way to make friends with groundlessness and the ever-changing energy of life, then we'll always be struggling to find stability in a shifting world. And old age and death will come as a terrible shock. No question, most of us are afraid of death, and there are downsides to growing old. You don't hear as well, your back hurts, you forget things. Younger people, if they notice you at all, see you as worn out, useless, over the hill, so your self-image is eroded.

As we train in the charnel ground, we discover that death is not an enemy and that aging doesn't have to be so daunting. I've found that age has lots of advantages. For one thing, I let go much more easily: knowing that it's all passing so quickly makes everything I encounter exceedingly precious. I know that every taste, every smell, every day, every meeting, every parting, could be my last. When I see people bent over, shuffling along on walkers, I know what could be ahead for me. I've begun to identify with the very elderly so intimately that instead of recoiling, I feel immense compassion.

As I move closer to death, I'm inspired to keep training in charnel-ground practice by this prayer from Dzigar Kongtrül:

When the appearances of this life dissolve
May I with ease and great happiness,
Let go of all attachments to this life,
As a son or daughter returning home.

The third commitment opens us to reality straight up. We're able to stay present with impermanence and death and with even the most frightening and humiliating moments of life. We're no longer looking for something other than right now, no longer looking for an ideal world. In the middle of the charnel ground, in the midst of the mandala of our life, we can finally contemplate groundlessness, impermanence, old age, sickness, and death, and be at ease with the thought: "This is just how it is. My old shirt won't last forever, and neither will I."

Concluding Words

At this time in history, we are to take nothing personally,
least of all ourselves. For the moment we do, our spiritual
growth and journey come to a halt. The time of the
lone wolf is over.

—THE PROPHECY OF THE HOPI ELDERS, 2000

11

We Are Needed

A T THE VERY LOWEST POINT in my life, when I was feeling utterly despondent, I started to see owls in the daytime. I would be in total despair, then look up, and there, sitting on the woodpile or in a tree or on top of the cliff, would be an owl—and it would wink at me. It always made me laugh at myself and go forward with a complete shift in perspective.

When life is hard, making a commitment to sanity can provide this same sort of wake-up call. When you're working with any of the Three Commitments, it will give you a fresh outlook precisely when you need it most—when you're on the verge of crashing.

So I leave you with a question: Are you ready to make a commitment? Is the time right for you to commit to not causing harm, to benefiting others, to embracing the world just as it is? Are you willing to make any—or all—of these commitments for a lifetime or a year or a month or even a day? If you feel that you're up for it, then start wherever you are and voice the commitment to yourself or to a friend or to a mentor or spiritual teacher. You make the commitment knowing that if you break it, you simply acknowledge that you broke it and start again.

Underlying the question of whether you're ready to make these commitments is a deeper question: Are you ready to embark on the journey of embracing the groundlessness of life? Are you ready to consider falling in love with the ever-shifting, never-certain reality of our situation? The Three Commitments as I've presented them are a support for losing our fear of groundlessness, for becoming intimate with groundlessness, for making friends with the fundamental ambiguity of being human.

The other morning I woke up worrying about a dear friend's well-being. I felt it as an ache in my heart. When I got up and looked out my window, I saw such beauty that it stopped my mind. I just stood there with the heartbreak of my friend's condition and saw trees heavy with fresh snow, a sky that was purple-blue, and a soft mist that covered the valley, turning the world into a vision of the Pure Land. Just then, a flock of yellow birds landed on the fence and looked at me, increasing my wonder further still.

I realized then what it means to hold pain in my heart and simultaneously be deeply touched by the power and magic of the world. Life doesn't have to be one way or the other. We don't have to jump back and forth. We can live beautifully with whatever comes—heartache and joy, success and failure, instability and change.

Groundlessness, uncertainty, insecurity, vulnerability— these are words that ordinarily carry a negative connotation. We're generally wary of these feelings and try to elude them in any way possible. But groundlessness isn't something we need to avoid. The same feeling we find so troubling when we open to it can be experienced as a huge relief, as freedom from all restraints. It can be experienced as a mind so unbiased and relaxed that we feel expansive and joyful.

Shantideva experienced it like this:

When real and unreal both
Are absent from before the mind,
Nothing else remains for mind to do
But rest in perfect peace,
From concept free.

But how does this shift happen? How can something we dislike so much become so soothing? The feeling itself doesn't change. We just stop resisting it. We stop avoiding the unavoidable. We stop struggling against the dynamic, ever-changing quality of life and instead settle back and enjoy it.

Chögyam Trungpa demonstrated the co-emergent nature of feelings in a teaching on boredom—on how we feel when nothing's happening. Hot boredom, he said, is a restless, impatient, I-want-to-get-out-of-here feeling. But we can also experience nothing happening as cool boredom, as a carefree, spacious feeling of being fully present without entertainment—and being right at home with that.

Similarly, the feeling of nothing to hold on to that we label groundlessness can switch from hot, queasy, disagreeable groundlessness, which we avoid, to cool groundlessness, which we find simultaneously invigorating and deeply relaxing. I call this positive groundlessness.

It's natural to want relief from the stress we feel when we encounter fundamental uncertainty—the uneasiness, the tension, the stiffness in the back or neck. There's no reason to reproach ourselves because we don't experience groundlessness as positive. In fact, while we're weaning ourselves off certainty, it's not a bad idea to have a degree of certainty for support. But how much of a security blanket do you need? Only you can answer that. Whatever you reach for—

the practices I've presented, a community of friends who are also on this path, a teacher you respect—you hold on to that security blanket only temporarily, with the aspiration to realize that ultimately there is no security blanket and with the intention to experience that realization as freeing rather than terrifying.

It's like the Zen Buddhist teaching that says you need a raft to get across the river, but when you arrive at the other shore, you leave the raft behind. You don't lug it around with you forever.

The difference in our story is that the raft never gets beyond the middle of the river. It floats along safely as we work with the first commitment but starts to fall apart with the second commitment and disintegrates altogether with the third commitment. By that time, however, having nothing to hold on to is no problem at all.

Chögyam Trungpa used to lead three-month retreats, and one year I served as the head of practice. My job was to make sure that the meditation hall was running smoothly, that everything was on schedule. I would be so pleased when everything was working like clockwork—and then Chögyam Trungpa would throw us off completely. If the regular afternoon talk was scheduled for 3:00 P.M., he would arrive at 3:00 on the first day, he would arrive at 4:00 the next day, and then on the third day, he would keep us waiting until 5:00. By the fourth talk, we were waiting until 10:00 P.M. Talk about groundlessness! The practice department didn't know how to set up a schedule. The cooks didn't know when to serve meals. After a while, we almost weren't sure if it was day or night.

This turned out to be the best sort of training possible for embracing the fundamental ambiguity of the human condition, the fundamental groundlessness of life. We can rant and rail all we want when our carefully laid plans are upset, when our schedules go out the window, when people don't show up when they say they will and show up when we least expect them. But at some point, we just have to give up and surrender to life, staying open to the unlimited possibilities of what—and who—might appear in our mandala.

The Three Commitments are exceedingly helpful props that support us in stepping into groundlessness. They offer guidance on what to do and what not to do and what to expect along the way. What they can't tell us is how it actually *feels* to progress along this path, what it feels like to shift from resisting groundlessness to embracing it. I thought of an apt analogy for this ineffable transformation: the experience of having dense cataracts removed from one's eyes. About a week after I had this procedure, I looked around, and seeing the world with my new, clear vision took my breath away. Visually, everything was stunning. I could use words like *vivid* and *vibrant* to describe the colors. I could use phrases like *sky larger* and *vistas huge* to describe the scenery. But none of those words, or any others I can think of, could adequately convey the sense of expansiveness I felt when I saw the brilliantly colored, multidimensional panorama. Until then, I hadn't realized how limited my vision had been.

That experience reminds me of a traditional Tibetan story called the Frog in the Well. One day a frog who had lived his whole life in a well received a visit from a frog who lived by the ocean. When the well frog asked how big the ocean was, the visitor said, "It's gigantic." "You mean about one-fourth the size of my well?" the well frog asked.

"Much bigger" was the answer. "You mean it's as big as my well?" asked the well frog incredulously. "Far bigger. There's no comparison," said the frog from the sea. "That's impossible. I don't believe you," said the well frog. So they set off together to see. And when the well frog saw the vastness of the ocean, it was such a shock that his mind couldn't comprehend it, and he died on the spot.

The journey through the Three Commitments won't be the cause of your death, but it will almost certainly leave you speechless. It can't be adequately put into words—my words or anyone else's. You simply have to experience it personally. You have to make this journey for yourself.

When we train in the Three Commitments, we find out what's possible for us as human beings. Taking each vow in turn and integrating what it has to teach us is something like going from being a toddler—eager, bursting with life, but not having much sense yet of what's ahead—to being a fully mature, complete human being living in a vividly unreal yet ever-present world.

In their prophecy of 2000, the Hopi elders said that in order not to be torn apart by these turbulent times, we have to let go of the shore and stay in the middle of the river, in the unceasing flow of life. But they didn't say we have to do this alone. "See who is there with you and celebrate," they said. "The time of the lone wolf is over."

Through the years, I've come to understand that even if I wanted to be a lone wolf, I couldn't be one. We're all in this together, all so interconnected that we can't awaken without one another. We need to help each other let go of the shore and stay in the middle of the river with no life jackets, no inner tubes, and no intention of ever clinging to anything again. The Three Commitments launch us on an exhilarating journey, a life-giving journey, a journey of appreciating one another and our unlimited potential for goodness.

The warrior's cry is: "We are needed." We make this journey for the sake of ourselves, our loved ones, our enemies, and everybody else. Since we all share the same planet, it's crazy to continue acting in ways that will destroy it.

May we all learn that pain is not the end of the journey, and neither is delight. We can hold them both—indeed hold it all—at the same time, remembering that everything in these quixotic, unpredictable, unsettled and unsettling, exhilarating and heart-stirring times is a doorway to awakening in sacred world.

Acknowledgments

To my primary teachers, Chögyam Trungpa Rinpoche, Dzigar Kongtrül Rinpoche, and Sakyong Mipham Rinpoche, I offer my heartfelt gratitude for all that they have taught me and for their patience with me.

To my loyal and dedicated secretary, Glenna Olmsted, and to Greg Moloney, I send my deep appreciation for helping me with the typing of this manuscript and for their ongoing kindness and support.

To my editor, Joan Oliver, I extend my profound thanks for taking the original transcripts of these talks and transforming them so skillfully into this book. It was indeed a pleasure to be able to work with Joan.

I also wish to express my gratitude to Dave O'Neal, my editor at Shambhala Publications, for his help and encouragement.

Related Readings

Brach, Tara. *Radical Acceptance: Embracing Your Life with the Heart of a Buddha.* New York: Bantam Books, 2003.

Chödrön, Pema. *No Time to Lose: A Timely Guide to the Way of the Bodhisattva.* Boston: Shambhala Publications, 2005.

Kongtrül, Dzigar. *It's Up to You: The Practice of Self-Reflection on the Buddhist Path.* Boston: Shambhala Publications, 2005.

_____. *Light Comes Through: Buddhist Teachings on Awakening in Our Natural Intelligence.* Boston: Shambhala Publications, 2008.

Masters, Jarvis Jay. *Finding Freedom: Writings from Death Row.* Junction City, Calif.: Padma Publishing, 1997.

Mattis-Namgyal, Elizabeth. *The Power of an Open Question: The Buddha's Path to Freedom.* Boston: Shambhala Publications, 2010.

Panchen, Ngari, and Pema Wangyi Gyalpo. *Perfect Conduct: Ascertaining the Three Vows.* Translated by Khenpo Gyurme Samdrup and Sangye Khandro. Commentary by His Holiness Dudjom Rinpoche. Boston: Wisdom Publications, 1996.

Patrul Rinpoche. *The Words of My Perfect Teacher.* Translated by the Padmakara Translation Group. Forewords by the Dalai Lama and Dilgo Khyentse Rinpoche. Boston: Shambhala Publications, 1994, 1998.

Saltman, Bethany. "Moral Combat," interview with Chris Hedges. *The Sun,* no. 396 (December 2008). Accessed at www.thesunmagazine.org/issues/396/moral_combat?print=all.

Shantideva. *The Way of the Bodhisattva.* Translated by the Padmakara Translation Group. Boston: Shambhala Publications, 1997.

Thubten, Anam. *No Self, No Problem.* Edited by Sharon Roe. Ithaca, N.Y.: Snow Lion Publications, 2009.

Trungpa, Chögyam. *Shambhala: The Sacred Path of the Warrior.* Boston: Shambhala Publications, 1984, 1988.

_____. *Smile at Fear: Awakening the True Heart of Bravery.* Edited by Carolyn Rose Gimian. Foreword by Pema Chödrön. Boston: Shambhala Publications, 2010.

Wheatley, Margaret J. *Perseverance.* San Francisco: Berrett-Koehler Publishers, 2010.

Books and Audio by Pema Chödrön

BOOKS

Always Maintain a Joyful Mind: And Other Lojong *Teachings on Awakening Compassion and Fearlessness*

In this book Pema Chödrön introduces fifty-nine pith teachings (called *lojong* in Tibetan) and offers guidance on how to make them part of our everyday lives. The book also features a forty-five-minute audio program entitled "Opening the Heart," in which Pema Chödrön offers in-depth instruction on tonglen meditation, a powerful practice that anyone can undertake to awaken compassion for oneself and others.

Awakening Loving-Kindness

Selected readings from *The Wisdom of No Escape,* presented in a small pocket-sized edition, perfect for carrying along in a purse, briefcase, or coat pocket. A portable book of inspiration on how to remain wholeheartedly awake and use the abundant material of daily life as your primary teacher and guide.

Comfortable with Uncertainty: 108 Teachings on Cultivating Fearlessness and Compassion

This book offers short, stand-alone readings designed to help us cultivate compassion and awareness amid the challenges of daily living. More than a collection of thoughts for the day, *Comfortable with Uncertainty* offers a progressive program of spiritual study, leading the reader through essential concepts, themes, and practices on the Buddhist path.

No Time to Lose: A Timely Guide to the Way of the Bodhisattva

In this book Pema Chödrön presents the traditional Buddhist teachings that guide her own life: those of *The Way of the Bodhisattva (Bodhicharyavatara)*, a text written by the eighth-century sage Shantideva. This treasured Buddhist work is remarkably relevant for our times, describing the steps we can take to cultivate courage, caring, and joy—the keys to healing ourselves and our troubled world.

The Places That Scare You: A Guide to Fearlessness in Difficult Times

We always have a choice, Pema Chödrön teaches: we can let the circumstances of our lives harden us and make us increasingly resentful and afraid, or we can let them soften us and make us kinder. Amid our difficulties, wisdom is always available to us, but we usually block it with habitual patterns rooted in fear. Beyond that fear lies a state of openheartedness and tenderness. This book teaches us how to awaken our basic goodness and connect with others, to accept ourselves and others complete with faults and imperfections.

The Pocket Pema Chödrön

Here is a treasury of 108 short selections from the best-selling books of Pema Chödrön, the beloved Buddhist nun. Designed for on-the-go inspiration, this collection offers teachings on becoming fearless; breaking free of destructive patterns; developing patience, kindness, and joy amid our everyday struggles; and unlocking our natural warmth, intelligence, and goodness.

Practicing Peace in Times of War

"War and peace begin in the hearts of individuals," declares Pema Chödrön. She explains that, remarkably, the way in which we as individuals respond to challenges in our everyday lives can mean the difference between perpetuating a culture of violence or creating a new culture of compassion. In this book Pema Chödrön insists that our world will begin to change when each of us, one by one, begins to work for peace at the level of our own behavior, our own habits of thought and action. It's never too late, she tells us, to look within and discover a new way of living.

Start Where You Are: A Guide to Compassionate Living

An indispensable handbook for cultivating fearless-ness and awakening compassion in the midst of daily living. Pema Chödrön frames her teachings on compassion around fifty-nine traditional Tibetan Buddhist maxims such as: "Always apply only a joyful state of mind" and "Always meditate on whatever provokes resentment."

Taking the Leap: Freeing Ourselves from Old Habits and Fears

In this book Pema Chödrön shows us how to break free of destructive patterns in our lives and experience a new sense of freedom and happiness. Drawing on the Buddhist concept of *shenpa*, she helps us to see how certain habits of mind tend to "hook" us and get us stuck in states of anger, blame, self-hatred, and addiction. The good news is that once we start to see these patterns, we can begin to change our lives for the better.

When Things Fall Apart: Heart Advice for Difficult Times
Drawing on traditional Buddhist wisdom, here is radical and compassionate advice for what to do when our lives become painful and difficult. There is only one approach to suffering that is of lasting benefit, Pema teaches, and that approach involves moving toward painful situations with friendliness and curiosity. This book includes instructions on how to use painful emotions to cultivate wisdom, compassion, and courage; how to communicate in a way that leads to openness and true intimacy with others; and how to reverse negative habitual patterns.

The Wisdom of No Escape: And the Path of Loving-Kindness
A book about saying yes to life in all of its manifestations, embracing the potent mixture of joy, suffering, brilliance, and confusion that characterizes the human experience. Pema Chödrön shows us the profound value of our situation of "no escape" from the ups and downs of life.

Audio

Be Grateful to Everyone: An In-Depth Guide to the Practice of Lojong
One of the best ways to bring meditation off the cushion and into everyday life is to practice *lojong* (mind training). For centuries, Tibetans have used fifty-nine powerful mind-train-

ing slogans as a way to transform life's ordinary situations into opportunities for awakening. In this seven-CD program, Pema Chödrön presents her definitive audio teachings on *lojong*. She offers an overview of the practice and goes on to provide inspiring commentary on the slogans while paying special attention to how to apply them on the spot in our daily lives.

Don't Bite the Hook: Finding Freedom from Anger, Resentment, and Other Destructive Emotions

In this recorded weekend retreat, Pema draws on Buddhist teachings to show us how to relate constructively to the inevitable shocks, losses, and frustrations of life so that we can find true happiness. The key, she explains, is not biting the "hook" of our habitual responses.

The Fearless Heart: The Practice of Living with Courage and Compassion

Pema shows us how to transform negative emotions like fear and guilt into courageous self-acceptance in *The Fearless Heart*. Her teachings are based on five aphorisms presented to Machig Lapdronma, one of Tibetan Buddhism's greatest female teachers. Here on five CDs, Pema offers insightful guidance on how to remain courageous in the face of pain and how to increase feelings of generosity and passion through fearlessness. This audio program includes an extensive question-and-answer session and guided meditation practices available for the first time.

Fully Alive: A Retreat with Pema Chödrön on Living Beautifully with Uncertainty and Change

In this recorded weekend retreat, Pema Chödrön and her teaching assistant, Meg Wheatley, teach us to stop clinging to the certainty of life's shore and to instead step right into the river; to be completely, fearlessly present even in the hardest times, the most difficult situations. It's the secret of being fully alive.

Perfect Just as You Are: Buddhist Practices on the Four Limitless Ones—Loving-Kindness, Compassion, Joy, and Equanimity

Here are Pema Chödrön's definitive teachings on the Buddhist practice called the Four Limitless Ones—a practice that helps us recognize and grow the seeds of love, compassion, joy, and equanimity already present in our hearts. This in-depth study course offers guided meditations, on-the-spot practices to use in the midst of daily life, an overview of *bodhicitta* and the Bodhisattva Vow, guided Shamatha meditation, writing and reflection exercises, methods to weaken the grip of negative emotions, and question-and-answer sessions.

Practicing Peace in Times of War: Four Talks

The book *Practicing Peace in Times of War* is based on several of Pema Chödrön's public talks, and we are proud to present them to you here, in this audio edition. It is a short, pithy, and profound work that includes practical strategies for cultivating the seeds of peace and compassion amid life's upsets and challenges.

Smile at Fear: A Retreat with Pema Chödrön on Discovering Your Radiant Self-Confidence

Behind each of our fears resides a basic fear of *ourselves*. In this recorded retreat, Pema Chödrön shares teachings inspired by the book *Smile at Fear*, which was written by her teacher Chögyam Trungpa. Here is a vision for moving beyond this most basic fear of self to discover the innate bravery, trust, and joy that reside at the core of our being.

Start Where You Are: A Guide to Compassionate Living

With insight and humor, Pema Chödrön offers guidance on how we can accept our flaws and embrace ourselves wholeheartedly as a prerequisite for developing compassion. Through working with fifty-nine Tibetan Buddhist slogans, Pema shows us how to develop the courage to face our inner pain and thereby discover a wealth of freedom, well-being, and confidence.

This Moment Is the Perfect Teacher: Ten Buddhist Teachings on Cultivating Inner Strength and Compassion

Lojong is a powerful Tibetan Buddhist practice created especially for training the mind to work with the challenges of everyday living. It teaches our hearts to soften, reframes our attitude toward difficulty, and allows us to discover a wellspring of inner strength. In this recorded retreat, Pema Chödrön introduces the *lojong* teachings and explains how we can apply them to any situation in our life—because, as Pema says, "every moment is an opportunity for awakening."

When Things Fall Apart: Heart Advice for Difficult Times

This abridged audiobook based on the beloved spiritual classic contains radical and compassionate advice for what to do when our lives become painful and difficult. Read by Pema, it includes instructions on how to use painful emotions to cultivate wisdom, compassion, and courage; how to communicate in a way that leads to openness and true intimacy with others; and how to reverse negative habitual patterns.

The Wisdom of No Escape: And the Path of Loving-Kindness

It's true, as they say, that we can only love others when we first love ourselves, and we can only experience real joy when we stop running from pain. The key to understanding these truisms lies in remaining open to life in all circumstances, and here Pema Chödrön shows us how.